HE & SHE

HE & SHE

60 SIGNIFICANT DIFFERENCES BETWEEN MEN AND WOMEN

Cris Evatt

CONARI PRESS
Berkeley, CA

Acknowledgements

Many people contributed to the writing of this book. My warmest thanks to:

Dave, my husband—for listening to all my "fascinating facts" about men and women, and for being so generous, good natured, and caring.

Susan Marie Schustak, my researcher—for providing me with up-to-date articles, books, press releases, and clippings about gender differences. Susan's commitment to assisting me in writing this book was integral to its content and finished product. Her enthusiasm knew no bounds.

Theo Gund—for promoting and believing in my books and ideas.

Mary Jane Ryan and Julie Bennett, my publishers—for their expertise and enthusiasm.

Candice Fuhrman, my literary agent—for her suggestions, encouragement, and humor.

Barbara Brauer and Stephanie Morrell—for their invaluable editorial assistance.

June Gresser and Sandra Healey—for letting me bring boxes of research materials and a computer into their office.

Others whose encouragement meant a great deal include Allyson Rusu, Mia Giles, Ev Dennison, Bruce Evatt, Susan Kirn, Patricia Nichols, Jacque Arabian, Paul and Evie Evatt, Kitti Cupp, Kathy La Rocque, Victoria Donald, Sid Morrell, Helen Strodl, Julie and Walter Grevesmuhl, Larry Bryant, Julie Jones, I.V. Peterson, Bernie Arthur, Lou Hefner, Connie Cox, Marti Rutishauser, John and Kathy Phair, Ryan Weerts, Joel Weerts, Dee Brueckmann, Betty Giles, and Jane Miller.

Contents

BEFORE
YOU BEGIN

Men and women are different. We all know that. But we are only beginning to understand just *how* different. "Only by regarding males and females as if they were two different species," says Tim Clutton-Brock, an ecologist from Cambridge University, "are we likely to understand why it is that the sexes differ so widely in anatomy, physiology and behavior."

Why are men and women different? No one knows for sure. Both biology and society play a part. But which contributes most is hotly debated. In the 70s, writes Christine Gorman in the January 20, 1992 issue of *Time*, "talk of inborn differences was distinctly unfashionable, even taboo." Differences were seen as socially based, a product of sex role conditioning.

Now the pendulum seems to be swinging in the other direction as "the evidence for innate sexual differences ... began to mount," claims Gorman. Anne Moir and David Jessel, the authors of *Brain Sex: The Real Difference Between Men & Women*, lead the way in this biological revolution saying, "the society we grow up in does affect us, but essentially in reinforcing our natural differences."

Other experts still believe upbringing has more influence than genes and that what is perceived as inborn is really residual cultural conditioning. Feminists such as Carol Tavris and Barbara Ehrenreich caution that using such biologically-based assumptions will once again limit the options women have and may have arisen as a reaction to the social changes women have instigated in the last 30 years.

I don't profess to have all the answers. Chances are the debate will continue to rage; what I've tried to do is give a balanced perspective, with both sides represented. The very fact of the differences is what intrigues me. My research into gender differences took place over a seven year period, following the publication of my book, *The Givers and The Takers*. While writing it, I became fascinated by the differences between men and women and collected every article and book I could find on the subject. I came to see that gender generalizations could accurately be made

6

and that much of what troubles us about the opposite sex could be traced back to a few fundamental differences.

I have come to see that gender differences often cause conflicts and confusion in love, work, and parenting relationships. "One of my first steps in therapy is to explain that the differences between men and women, if unrecognized, can lead to trouble," says Dr. Pierre Mornell in *Passive Men, Wild Women*.

The divorce rate hovers around 50 percent and there's no sign of a downward shift. "Misunderstood gender differences are one of the biggest causes of divorces," says Dr. Howard Markham, Director of the University of Denver's Center for Marital and Family Studies. It is my hope that by having gender differences clearly delineated in one concise volume, women and men will be better equipped to understand one another.

Degrees of Difference

With that said, a major caveat is needed. No man is like any other and no woman is either. Just as there are no two thumbprints, snowflakes or leaves that are identical, we are each unique, one-of-a-kind creations that will never be duplicated or repeated. Yet, underlying our uniqueness is a generality—our gender personality. To varying degrees, we have been stamped male or female. By understanding this personality, we will understand ourselves and each other better.

As you read this book, it's important to remember that the descriptions of women and men are generalizations. No one fits them perfectly. Your friend Barb may love sports and games (a typically "male" trait) while Rick is quite empathetic (a typically "female" trait). Moreover, you may find yourself coming up with examples of people who are blatant exceptions—men with overall more female traits and women with more male traits. Expect this to happen. Generalizations are averages—they tell you a lot about large groups of people, but very little about any one individual.

These gender differences also don't take class, race or ethnicity into account—again, they look at us through one lens, that which we call maleness and femaleness as defined by white Western culture. And it is important to understand that many of these behavioral traits are evolving as women and men explore what it is to be female or male.

Finally, while making generalizations can be dangerous, as Deborah Tannen, author of *You Just Don't Understand: Women and Men in Conversation* points out in *New Age Journal*, "It's women in particular who suffer if we don't describe the differences because we have one standard in this country—and that standard is based on men's way." Honoring our different perspectives is what *He & She* is about.

It's a Sourcebook

This book was written for women and men who juggle busy schedules and is designed to be used as needed. It's easy to pick up and put down because each topic is a two-page summary—a compilation of data from a variety of sources. Topics that were chosen appear frequently in magazines, newspapers, scientific journals, and on television talk shows.

Each of the 60 differences cites research that has been done, and offers quotable quotes and tips on coping with the opposite sex (or dealing with the issue in yourself). At the end of each discussion, you'll find a heading like "To Explore Further." Listed here are simple suggestions, books to read, movies to rent, and workshops to attend. Most of the books I've recommended were written for women because fewer are available for men. "More women than men read self-help books," notes psychologist Penelope Russianoff. "More women lead men to counselors or into therapy than the other way around."

Don't rely on any particular book, including this one. Each author is biased and highlights different points. By reading the work of several authors, you will get closer to the essence of maleness and femaleness.

This book doesn't urge women to become more like men, or men to become more like women. It's about retaining gender traits that serve us—both individually and

8

collectively—and modifying or dropping traits that do not. In *Self* magazine, Lyn Nesbit writes, "I long for a world in which men and women can easily and generously acknowledge their different perspectives and see how enhancing rather than threatening these differences can be." I heartily agree.

—Cris Evatt

How Well Do You Know Women and Men?

Here's a quiz on gender differences. Take it now to see how well you understand men and women. The answers are on page 154.

1. Women's language is more direct than men's. T__F__
2. Men seek assistance from others more than women. T__F__
3. Women try to change others more than men. T__F__
4. Men are more jealous than women. T__F__
5. Women boast about their successes more than men. T__F__
6. Respect is a major issue in the female world. T__F__
7. Men need more "space"—private time—than women. T__F__
8. Women respond better to stress than men. T__F__
9. Men seek approval from others more than women. T__F__
10. Winning through intimidation is a male skill. T__F__
11. Women are more decisive than men. T__F__
12. Men like to give orders more than women. T__F__
13. Women are more apologetic than men. T__F__
14. Men tell more jokes and stories than women. T__F__
15. Women usually dominate public discussions. T__F__
16. Men accept words at face value more than women. T__F__
17. Women take more physical risks than men. T__F__
18. Men talk about their feelings more than women. T__F__

19. More women than men are worriers. T__F__
20. Men would rather talk about things than people.
    T__F__
21. Women avoid verbal confrontation more than men.
    T__F__
22. Men nag—repeat requests—more than women.
    T__F__
23. Women interrupt others more than men. T__F__
24. Men gossip about others as much as women. T__F__
25. Women want to be married more than men. T__F__
26. Men talk on the phone more than women. T__F__
27. Women are more facially animated than men. T__F__
28. Men's posture leans toward others more often than
    women's. T__F__
29. Women have about one-tenth as much testosterone
    as men. T__F__
30. Men talk about health matters more than women.
    T__F__

THE
BASICS

♀♂
The Most Significant Difference

Women tend to be other-focused; men tend to be self-focused

Women see themselves primarily in relation to the people around them and their sense of self comes from this relatedness. Women habitually focus outward and have a virtually inexhaustible fascination with, and concern for, others and their needs. It's what makes women such good mothers, mates, and friends. Caring about and for others is such a strong female trait that a woman can even do it to the detriment of herself. A recognition of this is apparent in the popularity of the concept of codependency. "A woman's greatest challenge in a relationship is to maintain her sense of self while she is expanding out to serve the needs of others," writes Dr. John Gray in *Men, Women and Relationships*.

On the other hand, men tend to think, act, and feel in ways that show the self is primary and others are secondary. Indeed, as many researchers have shown, a man's sense of self comes from pitting himself against others in a process of individuation. This self focus enables a man to act in the world decisively and with self confidence. Therefore, to be close to others, men must travel a greater psychological distance than women. "A man's biggest difficulty is to overcome his tendency to be self-absorbed," says Gray.

Of course, individual men and women are best seen on a continuum. Women tend to be heavily, moderately, or lightly other-focused, while men tend to be heavily, moderately, or lightly self-focused. And some members of each gender act more like members of the opposite sex.

Which is better? Neither, although historically the male way of being has been valued and women have been seen as deficient. It's only recently that we've begun to ac-

14

knowledge women's ways as different, not inferior.

On a personal level, problems can arise when a strong sense of self is coupled with a weak sense of others; the self can become demanding and abusive to others. Similarly, if a strong sense of others is coupled with a weak sense of self, the self can become feeble, fearful, and easily trampled. It's best to have a balanced awareness of self and others.

Starting Young

The focus on others by females showed up in a fascinating study on perception done in the 70s. A group of children were given special binoculars that showed the left and right eye different images at the same time. They were all shown the same things, but boys reported seeing significantly more objects, while girls saw more people.

Quotable Quotes

• "I don't think boys in general watch the emotional world of relationships as closely as girls do. Girls track that world all day long, like watching the weather."—Carol Gilligan, psychologist

• "In any given society feminine personality comes to define itself in relation and connection to other people more than masculine personality does."—Nancy Chodorow, psychologist

What's Ahead

The female traits in this book confirm the general conclusion that women tend to focus on others more. Likewise, the male traits give concrete examples of how men's attention is primarily on the self. As you read, ask yourself, "How does this support the main premise?"

Your Own Journey

The best book I've found is *The Opposite Sex* (Salem House Publishers) by Dr. Anne Campbell, Associate Professor of Psychology at Rutgers University. It's an excellent reference, and colorful graphics and photos make it fun to read.

♀♂

Too Close for Comfort

Women need more closeness
and men need more distance in relationships

How many times have you read about or heard women complain about emotionally distant men? Words such as "cool" are used to describe men who put up "walls." The need to control distance with others seems to be a universal male trait. According to the authors of *Brain Sex*, "Men's impermeable and rigid ego boundaries make it difficult for them to permit the kind of intimacy that women take for granted."

Conversely, women are drawn ineluctably to people and tend to desire more closeness, connection, and intimacy in relationships than men. Even their posture leans toward others more than men's: in *Nonverbal Communication*, psychologist Shirley Weitz cites several studies showing that women tend to orient their bodies towards others much more than men.

Women's need for intimacy varies from woman to woman, as men's need for distance varies. Real problems arise when extreme clingers get together with extreme distancers. Or when women have unrealistic expectations about intimacy and men have unrealistic expectations about distance. "What's important is being satisfied with the amount of intimacy you have. Every relationship sets its own level of intimacy. There's no optimal level," says James M. Harper, Ph.D, family therapist at Brigham Young University.

Confirming Studies

Certain studies hint that men's need for distance may have a biological component:
• Notarius & Johnson (1982) tested the "skin conductance" of married couples while one partner complained and the other listened neutrally. The husbands showed much higher

skin conductance (a stress indicator) than their wives. The complaining of their spouse bothered men more than women. The increased arousal of the men's sympathetic nervous system suggests that men respond emotionally to complaining whether or not they respond verbally.

• Levinson & Gottman (1985) examined husbands' arousal level while waiting to speak to their wives about the events of the day. They found that the mere anticipation of intimacy is arousing (i.e., stressful) for men. They also found that arousal dissipates more slowly in men than women. Moreover, there was evidence that men's arousal level has more negative side effects, both physiological and psychological, than women's.

Do Either of These Sound Familiar?
Some men have an extreme need for distance which can manifest itself in one of two personality types. Fewer women fit either of these descriptions.

• **The Shake-and-Wakes** (Verbal Distancers): These men talk slowly, softly, and in a monotone voice. Like Clint Eastwood, they give short answers, and get verbally excited only if their pet subject comes up. These introverts often marry extremely talkative women. They are harder to get to know than the average man.

• **The Loners** (Space Distancers): These "confirmed bachelors" cannot live with women or male roommates. They may date a woman once or twice, or space dates weeks and months apart. They usually like sex, but if a woman stays overnight, she may have to leave after breakfast. His dog is often his live-in companion.

To Explore Further
• *The McGill Report On Male Intimacy* (Harper & Row) by psychologist Michael E. McGill will tell you more about men's compelling need for distance and women's need for closeness. McGill notes that some men try to meet women's intimacy needs by asking personal questions "as a way to forestall if not put off completely the need for one's own disclosure. One man acknowledged this use of listening to get close without 'getting too close.'"

♀♂
Advance or Retreat?

Men's biggest fear is engulfment, while women's biggest concern is abandonment

"I feel smothered!" Men's need for distance makes them sensitive to being engulfed by others. They can only handle a certain amount of closeness—talking, pampering, affection, being together—and if that amount is exceeded, they tend to pull away. However, most men don't know how to tell women when they feel smothered and need distance. They just unconsciously feel pressured and seek relief immediately. They may read the paper, go out with the guys, become silent or work late—anything to make some space.

Women often feel abandoned when men seek relief; their need for intimacy is thwarted when men distance themselves. Under stress, they tend to come towards men, asking for connection or comfort. Abandonment feelings— loneliness, sadness, desperation, anxiety, etc.—are a natural outcome of making others one's primary focus. If women define themselves by and through relationships, it is only natural that they suffer when men distance themselves.

Women also tend to blame themselves for men's behavior. Rather than understanding that such behavior comes from a deep-seated gender difference, they feel it is their fault: "He doesn't love me! What am I doing wrong?" However, women have not done anything "wrong" when men wish to distance themselves. It is really a function of this fundamental difference. As Carol Gilligan, author of *In a Different Voice*, writes, "male gender identity is threatened by intimacy while female gender identity is threatened by separation. Thus males tend to have difficulty with relationships, while females tend to have problems with individuation."

Different from the Start

In studies of young children, British researchers Diane McGuiness and Corinne Hutt have found:

• Infant girls as young as two to three days maintain eye contact with adults almost twice as long as boys.

• At four months old, most baby girls can distinguish photos of people they know from those of strangers; boys usually cannot.

• Preschool girls spend an average 92.5 seconds saying goodbye to their mothers at the school gate; boys spend about 32 seconds.

• A newcomer—of either sex—to school will tend to be greeted with friendship and curiosity by girls and indifference by boys.

So What Can We Do?

• **For women:** 1. Don't expect men to act like your women friends who need intimacy as much as you do. 2. Learn to recognize symptoms of men's feelings of engulfment. Smothered men act tense, tight, angry and make comments like "get off my back" and "lighten up." Then they retreat. Give men space and they tend to come forward. 3. Notice how men's engulfment feelings and actions provoke your fear of abandonment. Try not to take men's behavior to heart—it's not personal; by seeing it as normal, you may not be so afraid.

• **For men:** 1. Don't expect women to act like your men friends. Other men need distance as much as you do, but women crave closeness. 2. Begin to recognize your needs for distance and be willing to articulate your needs: "I really need to sit in front of the TV right now and be alone." 3. Recognize the symptoms of women's fear of abandonment: they may become highly emotional, loquacious, and worry about being loved. Short-circuit these feelings by being caring at the first sign of neediness. A simple, "I care about you even though I'm not with you all the time" can work wonders.

♀♂

Who Am I Really?

Women tend to over identify with people; men over identify with work

Many women put their personal interests and talents on the back burner in order to fill the needs and wants of their lovers, children, and friends. This has good and bad consequences. No one could be a good mother, for instance, without sacrificing at least some of her needs for her children's sake. But if she puts too much of herself into others, a woman can lose her sense of self altogether. As Louise Eichenbaum in *Between Women* says, "a woman's malleable boundaries create confusion about where she ends and another person begins."

Men tend to forget themselves in others much less frequently. Being primarily self-focused helps them keep more in touch with their own needs. For male identity is very strongly linked to personal actions, decisions, ideas, and facts, much more than women's. However, their needs are very tied up with performance and men can get so caught up in performance that they lose their sense of self.

Indeed, men's identities as doers can lead to workaholism and an abandonment of the self to work as profound as the female abandonment of self to others. "Of course, most men sell a good portion of their identity out to the institutions just as women sell out to a man," notes Warren Farrell in *Why Men Are The Way They Are*. In their frantic need to perform, they can lose touch with many other important things in life—friendship, solitude, love, childrearing. Lately, the men's movement has begun to address this issue as men get in touch with what they have had to sacrifice to succeed in the world.

It's So True!
• "The pillars of male identity are warfare, work and sex."—Sam Keen, psychologist

• "Women today have been sold a bill of goods by the male-oriented society which is stressing achievement rather than being." —Joseph Campbell, *This Business of the Gods*

Genderalizations

We've been talking about personal identity, but what about "gender identity"—masculinity and femininity? Generally speaking, the more self-focused a male, the more masculine—strong, virile, controlling, macho—he will appear. And the more other-focused a woman, the more acquiescent—weak, emotional, dependent, feminine—she will appear. In other words, the more out of balance people are, the more they become a caricature of their gender.

Dream More, Sacrifice Less

Many women would like to have a stronger sense of self. And it is up to them to forge an identity that can compete with their relationships. No one else can do it for them. In *Secrets About Men Every Woman Should Know*, psychologist Barbara DeAngelis says, "Each time you give up an interest, a friend, or a dream in the hope of winning a man's love, you give away a piece of yourself. The more you sacrifice, the less of yourself remains, until one day you wake up and you feel empty. There is nothing of you left."

Your Own Journey

• **Women:** For inspiration, rent the video "Shirley Valentine"—a married woman "finds herself" while vacationing in Greece. Also see "An Unmarried Woman" and "Private Benjamin."

• If you're a scholar, you'll like Ruthellen Josselson's book, *Finding Herself—Pathways to Identity Development in Women* (Jossey-Bass). Ordinary women, interviewed first as college students and then 12 years later, reflect on their life choices.

• **Men:** *Knights without Armor: A Practical Guide for Men in Quest of Masculine Soul* (Tarcher) by psychologist Aaron R. Kipnis teaches men to live rather than perform. Also see "City Slickers."

THE
INTIMACY
SEEKERS

She's a Pleaser

Women tend to seek the approval of others, while men do what they please more often

Approval is needing a favorable opinion from others, or getting permission to do something. Because of women's focus on others, they unconsciously tune into other people's approving and disapproving looks in order to please others and get what they want—which is to be liked and feel connected.

You've heard the song "I Did It My Way." Well, that's how most men do it. Most men are more concerned about attention and respect than approval. They don't like being told what to do. It makes them feel like underdogs, second-in-command, less manly. Men please less because, since they are self-focused, they are less afraid to have enemies, to engage in conflict, and to display anger. This means that they tend to do as they please.

Not all women are approval-seekers, of course. Madonna, Shirley MacLaine, Patricia Schroeder, and Whoopi Goldberg are just a few of the strong-willed women who have their own agenda. For many women, however, approval-seeking is a way of life. Writer Erica Jong confides, "On the outside I was a totally driven writer, but on the inside I felt that I would sell my soul for approval from a man."

Early Training

Beth Milwid, Ph.D., who wrote *Working With Men,* interviewed 125 professional women. Here's what one woman shared: "the whole thing of being liked is just not an issue for men. I remember that as a kid I'd go home and say `So-and-so doesn't like me.' And my mother, rather than say, "Screw her!" or "Screw him!" or "So what?' would say, `Now tomorrow, you go and tell this person that they look

24

very nice and they've done something very well. Give them a compliment.'" As this story shows, many little girls are taught to be very concerned about other's opinions.

Notable Quotes
• "Highly sensitive to criticism, I seemed to spend my life trying to do everything to please everybody. Consequently, not only did I not please myself, but I was so busy being what the other person wanted me to be that I almost assumed another identity." —Joan Collins
• "Women are taught to enhance other people at the expense of the self; men are taught to bolster the self, often at the expense of others. It's hard to get it all in balance." —Harriet Goldhor Lerner, Ph.D., *The Dance of Intimacy*

She Can't Say No
"Ever come away from the phone after having said yes to 48 dozen cookies for a Halloween party, the chairperson-ship of two committees, and extra work hours that conflicted with personal plans? Afterwards, you feel you could cut out your tongue, die or at least develop some highly contagious disease, " writes Sue Thoele in her very helpful book, *The Courage to be Yourself: a Woman's Guide to Growing Beyond Emotional Dependence* (Conari Press). "Feeling like that means you've just given yourself away." To stop, says Thoele, women must replace their draining shoulds with empowering words like *can, want to, choose to,* or *will.*

To Go Deeper
• If you'd like to learn more about people pleasers, why pleasers have low self-esteem, and why pleasers settle for small favors, read Dr. Kevin Leman's book, *The Pleasers— Women Who Can't Say No and The Men Who Control Them* (Dell).

It All Depends

Men tend to be more independent than women

Most men don't like being subjected to another's rule—they want to do things *their* way, without interference. Socialization to independence begins early—little boys fantasize about being Superman and King of the Mountain. "As men develop, there is implicit and explicit admiration given to those who become leaders and take charge," says psychologist Morton Shaevitz.

Conversely, a "little girl, while still quite young, begins to act in a different way from a little boy. Where he is independent and aggressive, she is coy and winsome. Her whole way of functioning is in relation to someone else from whom she may attract attention or care or love," says M. Esther Harding in *The Way of All Women*.

Women's primary need for intimacy creates dependence on others. It is women who depend more on phone calls from lovers, on being told "I love you," on being appreciated. It is women who suffer the most when others don't come through.

Men unconsciously sense that intimacy is women's Achilles heel, and that for many women, having *someone* is better than having no one—even if he's a rat. They instinctively know that many women have a hard time leaving destructive relationships because of their dependence on loving. Writes M. Scott Peck in *The Road Less Travelled*, "Dependency may appear to be love because it is a force that causes people to fiercely attach themselves to one another. But in actuality it is not love; it is a form of antilove."

Cinderella, Cinderella

In *The Cinderella Complex*, Colette Dowling says that women are brought up to have a hidden *fear* of independence. Two other sources suggest different reasons:

• **Survival is at stake:** In a hunter-gatherer environment, these behaviors made it possible for women and their children to survive. So say psychologists Glantz and Pearce in *Exiles From Eden:* "We disagree (with Dowling). A woman's reluctance to be independent is not based on a pathological fear; it is, rather, a genetic strategy designed to enable her to bond with the provider of meat. This strategy is mediated by the emotions: women get a feeling of discomfort and dissatisfaction when faced with being completely on their own."

•**Hormones are responsible:** "Both boys and girls whose mothers had taken extra male hormones during pregnancy were found to be more self-sufficient, self-assured, independent and individualistic on a standard personality questionnaire. Those who mothers had taken female hormones preferred group activity and were more reliant on others," say the authors of *Brain Sex*.

Men's Dependence on Women

Even though men are more independent, it does not mean they have no dependency needs. Indeed men rely a great deal on women's nurturance, support, and approval. In *Trusting Ourselves*, Karen Johnson, M.D., says, "Heterosexual boys grow up learning to depend on women—first mothers, later wives. We have a tendency to think of men as not having dependency needs because their needs are more successfully and quickly met—often without the man even having to acknowledge that he has them."

To Go Deeper

• This issue has been looked at in great detail in books on codependency, notably by Melody Beattie in *Beyond Codependency* and *Codependent No More*. Twelve-step groups dealing with codependence abound; check local newspapers.

♀♂

How Do You Feel?

In general, women are more comfortable expressing their emotions than men

"How do you feel about it, Jeff?" "Murmph!" It's commonly known that most men would rather act on their feelings than talk about them. Men are taught not to show feelings because it's unmanly, a sign of weakness: "Men are taught to suppress all emotions except, under certain circumstances, *anger.* They are taught to be cool and calm, particularly in difficult or dangerous situations," says psychologist Jonathan Kramer.

Women, on the other hand, tend to be able talk freely about most feelings and feel frustrated over men's reticence. Women respond *emotionally* to many things that cause men to shrug and grunt. In fact, many men think women have more emotional problems than men do, because women openly communicate their troubles and worries.

This dichotomy can cause many problems between the sexes. In *The New Male-Female Relationship,* Dr. Herb Goldberg describes a common scenario: "He is attracted to her emotional intensity. Her expressiveness makes him feel connected to her and very much alive and human. *Later* in the relationship, these same qualities are proof to him that she is irrational and unable to control herself."

A Matter of Wiring?

Many experts state that men learn to hide their feelings. Though this may be true, Anne Moir and David Jessel, the authors of *Brain Sex,* offer a different explanation. They maintain that women have "a more efficient brain organization for speech. This is located in the front of the left hemisphere, while the same function in male brains is found both in the front and back—a less efficient distribution." Therefore, they argue, it's actually harder for men to talk about their feelings because of the way their brains are constructed!

However, this doesn't mean that men can't learn to express their feelings. As Janice Juraska, biopsychologist at the University of Illinois at Urbana-Champaign observed in *Time*, "There's nothing about human brains that is so stuck that a different way of doing things couldn't change it enormously."

Reading Emotions
Studies show that women are not only better at expressing their feelings, but also at knowing the emotions of others. Shown photos of people portraying different feelings, women outscore men in guessing the correct emotion. They also can guess the emotional content of a garbled conversation better than men can.

Her Tears, His Tears
• **Women cry about five times more than men.** "Women have higher levels of the hormone prolactin, which is found in tears, and their tear glands are anatomically different than men's, possibly allowing them to tear more easily," says Dr. William Frey II, in *Crying: The Mystery of Tears*.
• **A hormone in men may actually suppress tears.** "Experiments with laboratory rats have shown that tear production is reduced when the animals are given high levels of androgen—the sex hormone that helps boys develop into men," reports *Woman* magazine.

To Explore Further
• **Women:** Most men can't handle an emotional outburst that exceeds 10 minutes. Carry a stopwatch. To understand men better, read *Why Can't Men Open Up* (Clarkson N. Potter, Inc.) by Steven Naifeh and Gregory White Smith.
• **Men:** Listen more to women when they talk about their feelings. They feel close to you when they talk—no matter what the subject. And remember you are being asked to respond in kind, not fix anything.

♀♂

Don't Worry, Be Happy!

Women tend to worry more than men

Women worry about everything more than men. They worry about serious things—nuclear holocaust and ozone depletion—as well as trivial—wrinkles and cellulite. They worry about their children and their friends, their mates and themselves. Worry researchers Thomas D. Borkovec and Janet M. Stavosky define worry as "a series of negative thoughts that intrude into the awareness in an uncontrolled manner." According to their study, published in *Women & Therapy* (Fall 1987), women are worriers at a rate of two to three times that of men.

Worry is a way of trying to get control over people and situations. It also is a way of being intimate with others; indeed the more other-focused a woman is, the more she worries about others. In *Why Women Worry*, Jane and Robert Handly say the primary worries of women are: relationships, financial concerns, personal appearance, pleasing others (or fear of not pleasing them), making the wrong decision, health, children's problems, not having enough time, growing old, job performance, parents, and world affairs.

Men would rather try to solve problems than worry about them. They want action. Men tend to be more pragmatic, matter-of-fact, and less emotional about most issues. "When men are concerned about an issue, they respond by either trying to solve the problem that's causing the worry or by distracting themselves," explains Harriet B. Braiker, Ph.D., who wrote *Getting Up When You're Feeling Down*.

Women tend to ruminate over worries. "Women are comfortable with being emotional. So instead of distracting themselves, they focus even more attention on their worries," says Stavosky. Some women resent men for not worrying about others' problems as much as they do. It suggests to them that men don't care. (This may or may not be the case.) On the other hand, many men feel women are worrywarts, which seems counterproductive to them—"Worrying never solved anything."

Fear Causes Worry

I went to an evening seminar several years ago that changed my thinking about worry. The speaker, Marshall Summers, asked the audience to give examples of fears. We came up with about 30. There was the fear of flying, spiders, snakes, bears, being alone, getting fat, losing a lover, going broke, and many more. Marshall looked at us and said, "All fears can be reduced to one fear--the fear of death."

How could that be? *All* of them? He gave an example. "You're afraid to fly because you think the plane will crash and you'll die." That made sense. He explained a few more. "You're afraid of being alone because without friends, you'll wither up and die. You fear going broke because without money, you'll be unable to buy food and shelter and you'll die."

I was convinced. Perhaps by dealing with our ultimate fear, women can give up worrying altogether--or at least so much.

Your Own Journey

Normal worrying shows caring and concern over problems we have or anticipate. Excessive worrying wastes time and energy, and may cause suffering—anxiety, sleepless nights, appetite loss, obsessive thoughts, and loss of concentration. When you begin to worry excessively, ask yourself:

• What do I *fear*? What is the root of my worrying?

• Have I done all I can to make the situation better? What else could I do?

• Should I seek professional assistance—a therapist, another medical opinion, an attorney, a carpenter, a cleaning service?

• Read *Why Women Worry—And How to Stop* (Prentice Hall) by Jane and Robert Handly for further help.

♀♂
Seeing Red

Men tend to express their anger; women tend to repress it

"Anger is a legitimate human emotion that can be expressed in one of three ways: passively, assertively, or aggressively," says psychologist Pamela Butler who wrote *Self-Assertion for Women.* "But in our society, women are not expected to express their anger in any way. Anger is, in fact, as much a `taboo' for women as sadness is for men."

Women are taught early on that anger is "unfeminine" and therefore unacceptable. "Dealing with anger is often difficult for women, since so many of us have been taught since childhood that it is not ladylike," say the authors of *The New Assertive Women.* Additionally, women so highly value their connections with others that they do not want to do anything that would break those bonds. In this sense, anger is very risky for women. Therefore, rather than blowing up in a straightforward manner, they tend to repress it, which can lead to depression and resentment or indirect expression--hinting, suggesting, complaining, and blaming. These are not very effective tactics for getting what you want. "Blaming," for example, "is a particular form of negativity that can be destructive in reducing motivation," says Dr. Irene Kassorla, Ph.D., in *Go For It!*

Men tend to be able to express anger directly because they are less concerned with alienating others. "To be angry demands a certain depersonalization of the object of one's rage—indeed, that person becomes an 'object', so fits more easily into the (self-focused) male mind set. Anger and violence demand a more abstract, impersonal view of the world—people become things to shout at and yell at," write the authors of *Brain Sex.*

32

Keeping It In

Psychologist Mary Kay Biaggio notes that when under verbal attack, men tend to become angry while women tend to feel hurt. When their needs are not being met, women typically know somewhere inside that they are angry, "but feel they should not express it. For some women this conflict manifests itself in the irrational fear of their own anger; they seem to fear that if they express the slightest amount of anger the floodgates will open and they will completely lose control."

Body Connection

Studies by Hokanson and Edelman show that even physiologically, men and women react differently to anger. When given a choice between a hostile counterattack, a friendly counterreaction and ignoring an attacker, men's blood pressure went down after counterattacking while women's blood pressure lowered only when making a friendly overture. Thus, for women, expressing anger was associated with anxiety and submission with relief. Hokanson and Edelman reasoned that such behavior was learned because if they punished the men for counterattacking, after several times they too learned to respond with anxiety when expressing anger.

Your Own Journey

• The best book on the subject is *The Dance of Anger: A Woman's Guide to Changing the Patterns of Intimate Relationships* (HarperCollins) by Harriet Goldhor Lerner, Ph.D. She teaches how to express anger constructively and notes: "Our challenge is to listen carefully to our own anger and use it in the service of change—while we hold tight to all that is valuable in our female heritage and tradition."

• Another good resource, especially in a crisis, is *The Angry Book* (Macmillan) by Theodore Isaac Rubin, M.D. Rubin covers anger from many helpful angles in short, easy-to-read chapters.

THE
COMPETITORS

♀♂

Applause, Applause

Men tend to seek attention more than women do

Both men and women enjoy attention, but for men, it's their lifeblood. Since they focus on themselves, they want others to do the same. Men attempt to attract attention in both subtle and obvious ways. They unabashedly talk about their achievements by telling stories about work and sporting adventures. They graphically describe their toys—cars, boats, planes, stereos, cameras, or scuba gear, to name just a few. They one-up each other in conversation: "Yes, but you should have seen how far *I* hit the ball."

The average women doesn't want to overtly upstage others. Since intimacy is her primary goal, she instinctively knows that attention-getting undermines intimacy. "We [women] cover up our excellence and competence because we are afraid to look arrogant and conceited to others," says psychologist Barbara DeAngelis. Instead, many women prefer the sidelines where they can applaud someone else's accomplishments. For applauding others is a form of nurturing.

Of course, this is changing as women become more focused on themselves. In *Male Chauvinism*, Michael Korda says, "Men have taken the easy way out, making half the species [women] their audience, looking out toward it for an applause which is becoming fainter and fainter, putting on a show that is already dusty with age." Women are no longer content to be on the sidelines, mere boosters.

Now, many women do seek center stage. Certain working women, professional female athletes, stage performers, and artists fall into this category. In general however, men still display more overt attention-getting behaviors than women.

Boys Will Be Boys

Researchers Whiting and Pope observed children in a variety of cultures. They recorded "attempts to call attention to oneself by boasting, or performing either praiseworthy or blameworthy acts with the intent of becoming the focus of another person's attention." They discovered that boys vie for attention more frequently than girls, and that sex differences are stronger between the ages 7-11 than 3-6.

Fashion Statement

"What a beautiful outfit! Where did you get it?" Of course, women do desire attention; often they seek it for what they wear. A chic haircut, a backless dress, or a new pair of earrings beg to be noticed. Women feel comfortable being recognized for their appearance because it is something that traditionally has been acceptable for women to be noticed for. Men, on the other hand, generally don't seek attention for what they wear, because it's what they do that counts most.

Starting Point

• **Women:** Study how men bring attention to themselves in conversations with others, then watch how often women tend to downplay their achievements. And if you tend to minimize your achievements, work on playing them up.
• **Men:** Observe the way women downplay their successes and how women's achievements often go unapplauded. Encourage women to receive recognition. You're a pro!

To Investigate Further

• **Don't hide your magnificence:** Read *Secrets About Men Every Woman Should Know* (Delacorte Press) by Barbara DeAngelis, Ph.D., a therapist and radio talk show host. "Women think that hiding their magnificence and acting humble is going to get a man to love them more, when in truth, this kind of behavior kills the passion in the relationship." DeAngelis encourages women to "make a list of their talents, abilities, honors, accomplishments, and good qualities, and share this list with your partner."

⚥

Is Winning Everything?

Men tend to be more competitive; women tend to be more cooperative

"The competition credo is accepted as the unspoken, unwritten and mostly unconscious contract that at once binds and divides men," says Perry Garfinkel in *In A Man's World*. Men constantly compare successes and accomplishments. When two men get together for the first time, the question "What do you do?" comes up immediately. Men measure everything from the size of their bank account to the size of their sex organ. "Evaluating oneself in constant comparisons with other men is a major characteristic of men," says Dr. Ken Druck in *The Secrets Men Keep*.

Because women focus primarily on others, they care less about winning and more about cooperating because competition threatens intimacy. When women do compete with each other, it tends to be covert. They don't jockey for status or rattle sabers as men do and feel uncomfortable acknowledging feelings of competition. Generally speaking, in men "the competitive thrust is overt and direct. With women, it's hidden from view, covered with a smile, a veneer of warmth and friendliness," explains Dr. Lillian Rubin in *Just Friends*.

It Starts Young
• According to Stanford researchers Maccoby and Jacklin who wrote *The Psychology of Sex Differences*, "boys' achievement motivation needs to be sustained or stimulated by competitive, ego-challenging conditions, whereas girls throughout the school years seem to maintain their achievement motivation more easily without such stimulation."

Women and Competition
• **Ancient roots:** In *Exiles From Eden*, Kalman Glantz and John K. Pearce write, "Women don't, as a rule, get the same

38

thrill out of winning a fight or staring down an enemy. Why is this? In the course of human evolution, winning fights was not the way females enhanced their reproductive success. Females who acted aggressively towards males weren't attractive to them, and therefore didn't have as many offspring."

• **Modern times:** Tennis champ Chris Evert is an exception to the general rule, proving that biology is not necessarily destiny. She learned to compete fiercely against others. "Winning made me feel I was *somebody*. It was like a drug. I needed the wins, the applause, to have an identity," says Evert. Indeed more and more women are becoming excited by competition.

Husbands with Successful Wives

Many women fear that success will threaten their relationships with men. These fears are not necessarily unfounded, but may not be true across the board:

• Psychologist Morton Shaevitz says, "Men find it difficult to deal with their wives suddenly becoming more successful than they are financially, achieving greater status and/ or visibility. Here the relative disparity tends to be experienced as *his failure* rather than her success. These feelings may be hidden and suppressed because they are embarrassing."

• In *Working With Men*, Beth Milwid, Ph.D., says, "Women who chose to involve their husbands in their careers reported a range of responses . . . . [but] The great majority feel proud of the way their husbands have come to grips with their careers."

Your Own Journey

Dr. Bruce Baldwin warns highly competitive men about the Competitive Compulsion which "interferes with your health and happiness, and abilities to relax and enjoy life." He suggests taking the ego out of competitive activities by doing the following:

1. Compete with yourself, not others.
2. Strive for improvement, not winning.
3. Learn to be yourself instead of performing.
4. Learn to play for the fun of it.

♀♂

Serious Money

Men are more motivated to acquire money and power than women

"Men will make the most extraordinary sacrifices of personal happiness, health, time, friendships, and relationships in the pursuit and maintenance of power, status, and success. Women won't; most of them are simply not made that way," says Anne Moir in *Brain Sex*. Power and money are symbols of manhood, proof of performance, quick tickets to applause, respect, self-confidence, freedom, and women for men.

Women, while interested in having money, tend to see it less as an extension of one's self and more as a medium of exchange. They enjoy the things money can buy—new clothes, home furnishings, exotic foods, and gifts. "Women tend to go into the market with clearer objectives and to see money for what it is—a tool. They understand that money buys things and security, whereas men tend to have an ambiguous view of money. They know it's a tool, but it's also an extension of their masculinity, a measure of how they are doing vis-a-vis other men," says Louis Rukeyser, host of PBS' "Wall Street Week."

Women have a different perspective on power too. "In the Female System, power is viewed in much the same way as love. It is limitless, and when it is shared it regenerates and expands. There is no need to hoard it because it only increases when it is given away," says Anne Wilson Schaef in *Women's Reality*. Conversely, men tend to see power as limited; the question is power over whom. Either you have it over them or the other guy has it over you.

Couples & Money
Victoria Felton-Collins, psychologist, financial adviser and author of *Couples and Money* (Bantam) notes these differences regarding money between men and women:

- **Fears:** Women fear becoming suddenly destitute: "What if I become a bag lady?" Men's fears are more specific and job related: "What if I'm injured? What if I'm laid off?"
- **Financial Self Confidence:** "Men appear to know it all, even when they don't. Women doubt they know it all, even when they do," says Felton-Collins.
- **Financial Advice:** When choosing an advisor, men tend to look at a person's track record and performance; women place more value on affiliation and trust.
- **The Blame Game:** When men score financially, they "attribute positive consequences to their own abilities ('I'm glad I saw that opportunity'); negative consequences to outside circumstances ('That damned stockbroker!'), notes Felton-Collins. Women attribute success to luck or their broker's good advice; negative results are their "own fault."

Fascinating Findings

- **Power-seeking can make you sick:** Princeton University psychologist John Jemmott III, Ph.D., measured the needs for power and affiliation (being with people) among 195 people. He found that people who had a much higher need for power than affiliation suffered depressed immune function under heavy stress, whereas those who placed a greater value on human relationships had increased immune function.
- **Female values:** Of 450 women entrepreneurs who filled out surveys for Avon Products, only 12 percent rated *profits* as the primary indicator of success. Ranked higher was self-fulfillment, job challenge, and helping others. "Women tend to have a broader definition of success. They don't define it totally in terms of money, which is refreshing," says Jill Johnson, spokesperson for the Minnesota Chapter of the National Association of Women Business Owners.

For Further Reading

- Get off the fast track and read *Success Trap* (Dell) by Dr. Stan J. Katz and Aimee E. Liu.

♀♂

The Respect Clause

Respect is a bigger issue for men than women

"I can't get no respect!" For many men, getting respect is as important as having power and money. Men tend to strongly identify with their achievements and want them to be admired—mainly by other men. According to Marc Fasteau, author of *The Male Machine*, most men's relationships with other men are about "respect but not intimacy." Wanting respect is a natural outcome of self-focus. The self who is acting in the world cries out for validation from others, which is what respect is.

How do you get respect in a man's world? By performing, of course! High adventures, sport triumphs, clever negotiations, financial successes, power over others, fixing things, and being witty and wise are a few ways men get respect.

In a woman's world, connection with others is more important than respect. Indeed, the very notion of respect is not one many women can relate to. It's not that women aren't achievers. It's just that they don't seek recognition for what they do as avidly as men do. "The game women play is 'Do you like me?' whereas the game men play is 'Do you respect me?'" writes Deborah Tannen, Ph.D., in *You Just Don't Understand.*

Teen Scene
• In a teenage boy's world, respected boys are considered "cool" while disrespected boys are "nerds" or "wimps." Here respect is largely based on how a boy talks, acts, and dresses. Teenage girls are less concerned about respect than boys (although what they wear is more important). Having close friends and sharing secrets rates higher.

Disrespectfully Yours
Many men don't respect women's way of being. That's

because traditionally, if a man were to exhibit female traits, he would be respected less by other men. Female traits are still considered "weak" in this culture and heterosexual men want to appear "tough" so that they will not be accused of being effeminate. This holds true, despite the changes that have occurred in the past 30 years.

• **Househusbands acceptable?** The majority of men still see respect in old, conventional terms. According to a recent poll in *USA Today*, 50% of the women and 60% of the men interviewed said they would not respect a man who stays home to take care of the kids while his wife works.

• **Women's way of knowing:** Today, many women are redefining respect for themselves, and coming to see that women's perspectives and ways of being have as much validity as men's. "The stereotyped male success pattern does not fit [women's] needs. Our journey is neither to dress like men, compete like men, or imitate men, using their definitions," says Ruth Ross, Ph.D., in *Prospering Woman.*

Quotable Quote
• "Men have to do some awfully mean things to keep up their respectability." —George Bernard Shaw

Your Own Journey
• **Listen for the word "respect" when men talk.** It comes up frequently—more often than either gender may think. The "R" word pops up in Mafia movies (check out "Godfather II" and "Goodfellas"), on sports programs, and in business conversations. War is also often about respect. Remember Saddam Hussein? He wanted it.

•**Listen to how women use the word "respect."** Most women rarely mention the need to be respected. Once in a while, you'll hear a woman complain about being disrespected by the man in her life or her children. The exception is in business. Here women are sensitive to men's lack of respect for them.

♀♂
What's Up, Jock?

Men usually have a greater passion for sports and games than women

"Who won?" Sports and games provide a showcase for male values. Here men can compete overtly. Winners get respect and attention; losers pledge revenge. And men can be with others without feeling pressured to be intimate.

Sports and games are ritual expressions of conflict. "Even in discussing and watching sports, [men] assume a combative stance. I have seen men with blood in their eyes while debating whether a ball landed in or out," writes Perry Garfinkel in *In a Man's World*.

Men like to talk about rules, strategies, and brilliant plays of the past—like the time Bill Mazeroski of the Pirates hit the ninth-inning home run that beat the Yankees in the 1960 World Series. Women's postgame chatter is minimal to non-existent.

In many ways, men define themselves as men through sports. "The intimate association between masculinity and athletics becomes glaringly clear when women try to join the game. If women can play, then, by definition, participation does not prove anything about masculinity," writes Marc Fasteau in *The Male Machine*. "Beating a woman proves nothing; losing to a woman is a major humiliation."

More and more women, however, are involved in sports. One example: In 1972, only 32,000 women competed in collegiate sports. By 1989, there were 130,000 women competing, reports *Time* magazine. But they do it differently—most women engage in sports primarily for exercise and companionship. Even when competitive, women's style is less flamboyant than men's. You rarely hear a woman cursing on the playing field or smashing a tennis racquet.

Child's Play
• **It's all in the game:** Researcher Janet Lever studied 181

fifth graders at play and reported these gender differences:
- Boys' games last longer than girls' games.
- Girls' play competitive games less often.
- Boys enjoy debates over the rules; girls are more apt to make exceptions.
  - If arguing occurs during games, boys want to repeat the play; girls often want to quit.
  - Girls like intimate play situations; boys like to play in large, age-heterogeneous groups.
- **Sports healthy for girls:** Researchers Mary Ellen Colton and Susan Gore found that girls who participate in some sport have higher self esteem and less depression than girls who don't.

Quotable Quotes

- "The games we [men] play in the office, at home, in the world at large, are merely devises to protect the fragility of our own egos." —Michael Korda, *Male Chauvinism*
- "Both war and sport are symbolic expressions of the same propensity . . . the theme of aggressive conflict between bonded, organized groups of men." —Anthony Stevens, *Roots of War*
- We seem to be ready for a greater balance between the games men play and the human equations women factor in." —Lynn Darling, *Self*

Facts & Studies

- According to a recent poll, the average male watches 6.8 hours of sports on TV per week.
- Researchers from the University of Tennessee found that triathletes who compete in "Ironman" marathon events were more egocentric and had less intimate relationships than average exercisers.
- Roughly 15 million people attend aerobics exercise classes; 95% are women, claims *Time.*

To Explore Further

- Look for *Manwatching* (Harry N. Abrams, Inc.) by Desmond Morris. This big book, with lots of photos, has an excellent chapter on the significance of men's sporting activities, which Morris calls "modified forms of hunting behavior."

COMMUNI-
CATION
GAP

♀♂

Subject Matters

Men tend to talk about things
while women talk mostly about people

"Girls are `person-centered' and boys are `thing-centered,'" says sociobiologist Leonard Benson. It's no different in adulthood. Men talk mostly about business, sports, and politics. About cars, gadgets, stereos and tools—about how things are made, how they work, how to fix them, how they effect the world. They eagerly exchange facts and opinions, as Dr. Ken Druck explains in *The Secrets Men Keep:* "Men are adept at talking about things rather than what they feel about those things."

Women talk mostly about *people*—people and their problems, people's reactions and responses. When women do talk about things, they are usually people-oriented: diets, home decorating, fashion, travel, cooking, hobbies, and health. Today, more and more women are talking about their careers, however, even a great deal of these work-related conversations are about people—how individuals work together, who's been slighted by whom, how best to create a smooth working environment.

Many men are irritated by women's highly personal subject matter: "How can I tell her I'm not interested in the lurid details of her friend's second divorce?" And many male topics bore women: "I don't care about X-331 drywall and 5/8-inch screws."

She's Expressive
According to linguist Robin Lakoff, women's language is very different from men's:
• Women often ask questions to keep conversations going; men regard questions more literally as requests for information.
• Women use more expressive adjectives like "gorgeous," "wonderful," and "incredible," more diminutives such as

"tiny," "cute," and "droplet," and more euphemisms such as: "I am not at all pleased that . . . " instead of "I am furious because . . . "
• Women use fewer colloquialisms than men.
• Women's conversational style is more collaborative than men's; men's tends to be competitive.

Remarkable Remarks
• "In almost every category from sex to money to food, the articles (in women's magazines) tend to have some psychological content . . . Men's magazines tend to stress performance—sexual, business, sports." —Dr. Joyce Brothers, psychologist
• Many subjects men talk about involve numbers. "Men— even men who scored lower on their math SAT's than Rwandan silverback gorillas—enjoy the firm security of numbers." —Colin McEnroe, writing in *Mirabella*.

How to Cope
• **Men:** Try to talk more about *people* when you are with women. Personal subjects may seem like a waste of time to you, but to women they're a source of great pleasure. Rely on your men friends for "thing talk." Tell your mate, "Honey, I'm getting together with the guys to talk about a thing or two."
• **Women:** Talk more about *things* when you are with men. You may not find facts as interesting as people, but you can learn to love them. Rely on your women friends more for "people talk."

To Investigate Further
• *You Just Don't Understand: Women and Men in Conversation* (Ballantine Books) by Deborah Tannen, Ph.D., is an excellent book on gender differences in communication. "This book could be the Rosetta Stone that at last deciphers the miscommunication between the sexes," says columnist Ruthe Stein of the *San Francisco Chronicle*.
• Another good book is *Talking Power: The Politics of Language* (Basic Books) by Robin Tolmach Lakoff, professor of Linguistics at the University of California, Berkeley.

♀♂

Talking Heads

Women tend to talk more in private; men dominate conversation in public

"Why can't men open up when we're alone?" says she. He, on the other hand, wants to be understood by the woman in his life without having to talk so much. "In the world at large men speak freely; in their private lives they fall strangely mute," explains writer Perry Garfinkel.

In private, men talk less than women because they are more comfortable talking about things, not feelings, and the intimate circumstance encourages women's way of communicating. Consequently, if conversations get too lengthy and emotional, men retreat. As author Joe Tanenbaum explains, "While women sometimes express to express, men almost always express to resolve . . . . Over time, men tend to become less communicative than they were in the beginning of the relationship because there seems to be no end to a woman's need to communicate."

This difference is profoundly felt in marital conflicts. Many women feel, "The marriage is working as long as we can talk about it," while husbands tend to think, "The relationship is not working if we have to talk about it," says Dr. Aaron T. Beck in *Love Is Never Enough*.

The verbal situation is reversed in public. Men tend to dominate meetings and classrooms; their language is less tentative then women's, and women often hesitate to express themselves when men are present. Moreover, men enjoy being the center of attention more than women.

Seizing Air Time
Study after study finds that men talk more at meetings, in mixed group discussions and in classrooms. Two examples:
• Catherine Krupnick, Ed.D., a Harvard education re-

searcher, studied classroom dynamics at Wheaton College. Her findings:

- Men have a shorter response time—their hands go up faster.
- Men's contributions tend to last longer.
- Men are less put off by disagreement.
- Men did 1/3 to 1/2 the talking, when they made up just 2/9 of the class.

Krupnick concluded that women should be encouraged to speak up in proportion to their representation in class, and men should be more sensitive to giving women a chance to speak.

- Communication researchers Barbara and Gene Eakin studied university faculty meetings. They found men talked more often and for a longer time—10.66 seconds to 17.07 seconds versus 3 to 10 seconds for women. The longest women's contribution was shorter than the shortest men's!

Couplestalk
When two couples get together, the men often dominate the conversation while the women sit back and listen. (Of course, some women chime in better than others.) Men dominate because they are more aggressive and they consider their topics more valid, whereas women have been socialized to "be nice" and let men talk about what they want.

How to Cope
- **Women:** Do you come on too strong verbally to your mate when he comes home after hectic day at work? *Passive Men, Wild Women* (Ballantine Books) by Dr. Pierre Mornell warns against engulfing men at this time.
- **Men:** In private, be patient with women's need to talk for the sake of talking—to exchange emotions and feel intimate. There doesn't always have to be what you would consider a point. In public, if you tend to dominate when women are present, back off a notch.

♀♂

Searching for Meaning

Men take words at face value
while women search for hidden meanings

Men tend to accept things at face value, to "cast things as either black or white," suggests Perry Garfinkel. They interpret words more literally than women do and are more matter-of-fact. Men usually "say it like it is"—unless they are conning someone—and often wish women would do the same. "Why can't she stick to the point?" they wonder when women go off on what to men seem like verbal tangents.

Women, on the other hand, like to delve into the meanings of human actions. They like figure out the mechanics of human behavior, just as men like to figure out the whys of outboard engines, football games, and business deals: "Why does Sue pick abusive men over and over?" "What is the real reason Fred left Alison?"

Men are often driven crazy by women's propensity to come up with reasons for human behaviors. From their point of view, reasons are not reality and they don't change an outcome. So why "wallow" in them? "Women, as a rule, have a greater fondness for talking things over. They have the compulsion to discuss all aspects of interpersonal problems which men often shun, sometimes with justification," states Dr. Karl Menninger in *Love against Hate* (spoken like a true man).

Proving the Point
• "Women think about men too much ... They have to talk about the nature of *relationships*. Most of the time, they analyze men into dust." —Pete Hamill, writer
• "What [men] find worth telling are facts about such topics as sports, politics, history, or how things work. Women often perceive the telling of facts as lecturing which not

only does not carry [for them] a metamessage of rapport, but carries instead a metamessage of condescension: I am the teacher, you're the student. I'm knowledgeable, you're ignorant." —Deborah Tannen, Ph.D, *That's Not What I Meant*

Your Own Journey
•**Women:** Try to take most things men say at face value. Don't look for hidden meanings (unless you think he's having an affair). What he says is usually what he means.
• **Men:** Have patience with women's need to analyze what others say and do. Sharing their revelations allows women to feel intimate with you. Don't belittle or discredit women's conversational style; appreciating our differences is the name of the game.

A Historical Perspective
• *Exiles From Eden* (W.W. Norton & Company) by Kalman Glantz, Ph.D., and John K. Pearce., M.D. gives an evolutionary perspective on men's and women's behaviors. To fully understand human behavior, one must go back to the days when we were hunters and gatherers, and understand our traits by studying data derived from archaeology, anthropology, and biology. The authors say, "If men and women understand how they are different, they will have a better idea of what they can expect from one another. We can no longer rely on chance and tradition to bring about understanding."
• *The Anatomy of Sex and Power: An Investigation of Mind-Body Politics* (William Morrow and Company, Inc.) by Michael Hutchison will also take you on a historical gender journey. He writes, "The human system appears to be approaching a bifurcation point, to be about to collapse into chaos or reintegrate at a higher level of complexity, interrelatedness, and order."

♀♂

Overt Versus Covert

Women's language tends to be more circumspect; men's tends to be more direct

Women are often accused by men of not being straightforward in their communications, of being sneaky or manipulative in the ways they speak. Because men have been dominant in our society, with most of the power and money, women have historically had to use language circumspectly to get what they wanted. On the other hand, "Men's language is the language of the powerful. It is meant to be direct, clear, succinct, as would be expected of those who need not fear giving offense," writes Robin Lakoff, Ph.D., in *Talking Power*.

From the female perspective, often men aren't circumspect enough; they can appear to women to be proverbial bulls in the china shop, verbally trashing everything in sight: "That's the stupidest comment I ever heard"; "No one in their right mind would do that." Women bristle at such a direct confrontational style, preferring language that is more inoffensive and connecting.

When men are indirect, it's usually about personal matters. Linguist Deborah Tannen explains, "When trying to negotiate mutual preferences and decisions, women are often more indirect than men. But when it comes to talking about their personal relationships and feelings, many men are more indirect."

Too Much of a Good Thing

Female linguistic diplomacy can be extremely helpful. But when it gets carried away, it can be self deprecating and destructive. Here are some of women's overly cautious approaches:

• **The politeness ploy:** Saying, "Are you sure it's all right with you . . . ?" rather than straightforwardly stating your desires.

• **Covert criticism:** Criticizing others by making suggestions like "You know it would be great if you would make five more sales calls a day," instead of calling someone directly on his or her actions.

• **Questions, questions:** Prefacing ideas with *questions*— "What would you think if we were to . . . ?"—rather than coming out and stating your opinions.

Assertiveness Conundrum

Linda Carli, Ph.D., assistant professor of psychology at the College of Holy Cross in Worcester, MA, studied the speaking style of 238 males and females. She found that women's talk was more tentative, deferential, and less confident than the men's because it is riddled with the following:

• **The disclaimer:** A prefatory comment or phrase that weakens the following statement: "I'm not sure, but . . . "

• **The hedge:** Weakens an idea by including words like "maybe" and "sort of." For example, "It's *kind of* snowing."

• **The tag question:** An undermining phrase at the end of a statement: "People should go to the dentist twice a year, *don't you think?*"

Carli found that the women in her study came across as less competent and knowledgeable than they really were—and that men liked women's language that way! Men don't like women to be too assertive or pushy, because assertive language and behavior violates men's standards for female behavior. "Low-status persons (in this case, women) must first demonstrate that they have no desire to compete for status before their ideas will be considered by higher status individuals," observes Carli. Thus, tentative talk is less threatening to men.

Writer Francine Prose read Carli's study and concluded, "Why not speak up, plainly say what we mean and recklessly hope for the best? In the long run, it may help men get accustomed to hearing what (assertive) women sound like."

♀♂
Play It by Ear

Women tend to be better listeners than men

"Uh huh." "Yeah." "Hum." "Wow." "Really?" Because women are other-directed, they tend to listen to others better than men. Studies have shown that women make more listening noises than men, and that women also acknowledge what others say by nodding and smiling more. Men are not as facially or verbally expressive when they listen and often control conversations with long silences and grunts designed to turn the conversation back to themselves or their interests.

According to linguist Deborah Tannen, when men lecture women, women generally listen. However, when men are in the listening position, they often challenge the speaker by changing the subject and offering their own information. In other words, *men struggle for control of conversations.* They don't want to be the listeners for long because, to them, the listener is one-down and the speaker is one-up. Men compete for the higher status of being speaker. Tannen explains, "Since women seek to build rapport, they're inclined to play down their expertise rather than display it. Since men value the position of center stage and the feeling of knowing more, they seek opportunities to gather and disseminate factual information."

When women talk with one another, listening is as desirable as talking because women want to feel intimate with the other. Women are eager to hear one another's story and validate one another by offering examples of similar experiences: "I know how you feel; I dated a guy like that ... " Women seldom challenge each other's information, because precise figures and facts don't play a pivotal role in their conversations.

Listening is an art and very few people of either sex in this society listen particularly well. "We often interrupt

56

other people before they have finished speaking. And frequently we tune them out long before we interrupt, because we are busy preparing our response," notes Dr. Gerald Jampolsky in *Goodbye To Guilt*.

The Interrupters

Two studies show that men interrupt more than women, especially if it is a woman speaking, and that this behavior is socially conditioned:

• **Kids videotaped:** Sociolinguist Julia L. Evans at the University of Michigan videotaped 10 four-year-olds and 20 eight-year-olds as they talked with women and men interviewers. The interruptions rates of the four-year-olds were the same. When the eight-year-olds were with male interviewers, the boys interrupted as often as the girls. But when this age group talked to the female interviewer, the boys interrupted 20 percent more often than any of the girls did. "I suspect the boys would have interrupted even more if they were talking to a female peer," says Evans.

• **Adults analyzed:** In a study by UCLA sociologists Candace West and Don Zimmerman, when talking to women they had just met, men interrupted 75 percent of the time. With women they knew, men butted in 96 percent of the time. Not only did they interrupt, but men often changed the subject to ones they preferred.

How to Cope

• **Women:** When you're in public, don't be afraid to challenge men who lecture you. Hone your speaking skills by reading *How To Talk So People Will Listen* (Harper & Row) by Sonya Hamlin.

• **Men:** Encourage women to express themselves in public. At home, try to be a more responsive listener. Grunts and silences don't cut it with women.

• Dr. Aaron T. Beck, author of *Love is Never Enough*, offers this suggestion: "Speaking without getting feedback is like talking to a wall. If you are the silent type, it may be helpful to get into the habit of giving nonverbal feedback, and not leaving your mate wondering whether you are really listening."

♀♂

To Do or Not To Do

Men are generally more decisive than women

"He who hesitates is lost" goes the [male] maxim. Warriors are decisive on the battlefield, and businessmen are decisive in the board room. According to the authors of *Brain Sex*, "the masculine ethos of management insists on blunt decisions—echoing the linear organization of their [men's] intellectual processes."

Women take more time with decisions because they take the human dimension more into consideration. Whether at work or at home, they want to figure out how this particular choice will affect not only themselves, but those around them. Women like to explore all the possibilities and get in touch with their feelings. They like to ask questions and get details: "I went to five stores before I found the perfect gift for Ginger!" Women don't mind shopping for options, whereas most men, in general, don't like to shop, even for solutions.

Women also consult others more. "Because women are more relationship-oriented, they tend to include others in the decision-making process," explains Dr. John Gray, the author of *Men, Women and Relationships*. Men tend to decide alone. "First, a man makes his decision privately in his `cave,' and then checks it out with others. If his conclusion is not accepted, then it's back to the drawing board."

Did I Do the Right Thing?
Women, more than men, tend to anguish over decisions after they have been made. They may worry that their decisions will hurt others or cause disapproval. "We're afraid the wrong decision will deprive us of something—money, friends, lovers, status—or whatever it is that the right decision is supposed to bring us," says author Susan Jeffers. As a result, women find criticism of their decisions hard to take.

In contrast, many men are open to feedback after they have made a decision. They don't mind being challenged. Women tend to think men's decisions are carved in stone because of their concise, forceful, self-directed mannerisms. (And sometimes they are!)

Team Approach

"We've always been a team on whatever we do. I don't think either one of us thinks of going out and making a decision without the other," says former First Lady Nancy Reagan. Not all couples get along as blissfully as Ronnie and Nancy do. Many women complain that their husbands make all of the major decisions and leave them with the minor ones. These men want control and tend to chose wives or girlfriends who are passive. Of course, in many marriages control for major decisions is shared, especially when a wife works. Economic power is a determining factor in modern marital decision-making.

Tips on Balanced Decision-Making

• View decision-making as an opportunity to learn.
• Asking the right questions is usually more important than coming up with the right answers.
• Become informed of the facts, but also get in touch with your feelings.
• Know your priorities. Make good big decisions and worry less about smaller matters.
• Seek help if it's needed, but know when not to take advice.
• After you've made a decision, don't fret over alternatives. If your decision turns out to be wrong, reverse it, when possible. We all make mistakes.

Further Resources

• *Overcoming Indecisiveness* (Avon) by Theodore Rubin, M.D.
• *Feel the Fear and Do It Anyway* (Fawcett) by Susan Jeffers, Ph.D.

♀♂

Heard It Through the Grapevine

Gossiping about others has different meanings and purposes for men and women

"Men and women dish out the dirt differently. For men, gossip is a game. The goal: to score points or just play. For women, gossip is a morality play that allows virtuous actors to set things right," writes Marilyn Elias in *USA Today*. Gossip also gives women a way to become intimate and involved in others' lives. It offers an escape valve for resentments and troubles, and is a way to gather information.

What do women discuss most? Men! "One noticeable difference in male and female gossip is that men say very little about their wives, whereas husbands are frequently the topic between women," says psychologist Michael E. McGill. Talking about men is an ancient female ritual and women will do it whether men like it or not.

When men gossip, it usually isn't about people's personal lives. Men rarely gossip about people's health, marriages, divorces, or children. It's about work relationships. They perk up over rumors about promotions, transfers, job performance, and what the boss is thinking. Inside information makes a guy look smart.

Men take pride in being what they consider to be discreet. "While women assuredly feel violated when their deepest confidences are revealed, men feel violated when *anything* is revealed, from their middle name to their preference in salad dressing," says Jean Gonick in *Glamour*.

Scuttlebutt Story

The gossip patterns of 350 men and women were studied by Donald Sharpsteen, a University of Denver psychologist. Some key findings:
- Men don't take gossip as seriously as women.
- If women thought gossiping was wrong, they stopped;

men didn't.
- Retribution is a powerful motive for women's gossip. Rather than expressing anger directly, women gossip about those they are mad at.
- Powerless men get off on "delivering the goods" on others to get attention.

Fast Friends

Gossip is one important way women connect to one another. A friend related this story to me: "Last night, a woman selling Shaklee products dropped by my apartment. I had met her recently over the phone. Before she left, I knew about her two divorces, current husband, minor surgeries, alcoholic family members, dyslexic child, and vacation plans. We shared back and forth for about an hour. When our conversation ended, we felt like best friends."

The Daily Schmooze

Studies show that women typically make three times as many personal phone calls as men and the average conversation lasts 20 minutes. Also, women don't need a particular reason to call beyond keeping in touch. Men, on the other hand, phone only when they have to convey information; the average male call lasts only six minutes.

Catty Comments

- "I don't have much respect for other women, and much prefer men. Men don't gossip or get catty." —Tracy Ullman, actor
- "The only reason that men don't gossip is that they seldom think for long or deeply about other people. Their main topics of conversations are money, politics, and sport." —Quentin Crisp, Lear's
- "Not everyone will admit to gossiping, let alone defend it. It's perceived as nasty, shallow and trivial, the aerobics of idle minds."—Aimee Lee Ball, Mademoiselle

♀♂
Advice or Sympathy?

When it comes to people's problems, men tend to give advice while women give empathy

Much has been written about women's frustrations with men when interpersonal problems arise. According to psychotherapists, when women go to their mate with an emotional problem, most men want to solve it immediately with a concrete proposal: Lonely? Make new friends. Frustrated at work? Speak up or find a new job. Bored? Find a hobby. The male solution is usually to take some action and so when confronted with another person's problem, they tend to prescribe action.

So what's the problem? Well, women often want *empathy*, not answers. In *Love Is Never Enough*, Dr. Aaron T. Beck says, "Men tend to hear women who discuss problems with them as requesting solutions, rather than looking for a sympathetic ear." Women may just want to be heard and/or held and told they are loved. Or they may want to talk the problem out, elaborating on the details of the situation before coming to a conclusion.

In a woman's world, empathy is highly valued. Women like both to give it and receive it. Most men, in contrast, tend to avoid a great deal of empathizing because they want to keep a distance from other peoples' personal problems to prevent themselves from feeling engulfed. Because of this, men will often change the subject when women bring up personal problems. It's a form of self protection.

Women tend not to feel as engulfed by the problems of others; indeed, heavy involvement feels natural: "Sensitivity to the needs of others and the assumption of responsibility for taking care lead women to attend to voices other than their own and to include in their judgements other points of view," observes Carol Gilligan, Ph.D., author of *In a Different Voice*.

Additionally, "Men tend to be more analytic, extracting the essential from the circumstantial detail. Women take in the larger picture," explain the authors of *Brain Sex*. Women bring in "an extra element of emotional sensitivity into the equation." In other words, women consider not only the facts of another person's problems, but his or her feelings about it as well as those of any other people in the picture. To many men, such emotional considerations are superfluous. Practical and solution-oriented, men feel responsible for taking action that will have an effect on and in the world. Therefore, focusing just on the facts allows them to create solutions that can be implemented without considering each and every emotional consequence.

How to Cope

• **Women:** When you want empathy and not solutions, tell your lover, "Honey, your solutions are terrific. But right now I need to talk about the problem and express my feelings."

• **Men:** When a women is feeling emotional over a pressing personal problem (that may or may not include you), try to figure out what she wants. It's often one of these:

A. She is upset, wants empathy now, and advice some other time—maybe never.

B. She is upset, wants empathy now, and solutions after she expresses her feelings.

C. She is not upset and wants to discuss a solution.

Further Resources

• *Men Are from Mars, Women Are from Venus: A Practical Guide for Improving Communication and Getting What You Want in Your Relationship* (HarperCollins) by John Gray, Ph.D., will help you understand gender differences with fresh eyes. For information on his seminars in major cities, write to John Gray Seminars, 20 Sunnyside Ave., Suite A-13, Mill Valley, CA 94941.

♀♂

Putting Up with Put-Downs

Men engage in verbal put-downs
more often than women

"Ooooh! That's hitting below the belt!" A put-down is a potentially humiliating remark or snub that, especially in public, attempts to injure a person's self-respect. Some are humorous, others serious. Successful put-downs are button-pushers.

Put-downs can be competitive—a way to score points. And quick jibes help men jockey for power, yet keep a distance. Believe it or not, put-downs bond men together— just think of TV "roasts" where celebrities get together to put down the guest of honor. "Men instinctively know that if a man can be teased about his body, his style, and his attitude, and laugh about it, he must have a strong self-image. He can be trusted," says Joe Tanenbaum in *Male & Female Realities*.

Most men only badger men they like. Bruce Kamen, the operations manager of KGO radio in San Francisco, puts it this way: "Those you like, you agitate. Those you don't, you ignore." Men put down women less frequently because women are uncomfortable with put-downs. Women want to be liked, not humorously or maliciously maligned and so they don't take kindly to such behavior. And they can also be very uncomfortable when men do it to each other in their presence.

Women are no angels! They put others down, too—but seldom to their faces. Women, being less confrontational, attack indirectly. They prefer backbiting to a frontal attack: "Did you hear what she did ... ?" By definition, a true put-down is a face-to-face event.

"On the average, men think it is funnier when a male disparages someone else than when he disparages himself, but women generally prefer self-deprecating humor," notes psychologist Carol Tavris.

Revealing Reasons

Male sibling rivalry often leads to vicious put-downs. For example, Jason and Mark, brothers two years apart, put each other down about 70 percent of the time they are together. I asked both boys, "Why do you put each other down so much?" Here were their answers: "I don't" (denial); "I like to see what he'll do" (seeking a reaction); "Because he's my brother" (sideways expression of closeness); "I believe what I say to him" (taking it literally); "For competitive reasons" (a keen insight.)

Female Coping Techniques

• **Tease back:** Dr. Adele Scheele, who wrote *Skills for Success*, teaches women how to get along with men in business settings. "When men tease each other, it's about power: *Can you one-up me? Are you strong enough to take it?* But when a man teases a woman, she sees it as an attack on her vulnerable spot: *He doesn't think I'm smart enough.* If she accepts the challenge, however, and reasserts her power by teasing back, she both shuts him up and earns his respect," explains Scheele.

• **Attitude is everything:** "Any woman who can interact comfortably and easily with the aggressive humor of men in business is one step ahead of the woman who negatively interprets these interactions," says Joe Tanenbaum. "Obviously this doesn't imply that women or men should put up with deliberate insults, chauvinistic attitudes, or racist remarks for the sake of being on the team."

To Go Further

• Tama Starr's *The "Natural Inferiority" of Women: Outrageous Pronouncements by Misguided Males* (Poseideon Press) is a clever compendium of male put-downs of women. Starr deftly guides us from Dr. Freud to Dr. Spock, from Moliere to Mailer, from Homer to Hemingway.

♀♂
I'm Sorry, So Sorry

Women apologize more than men

An apology is an expression of regret for having wronged another. Women admit to wrongs more often then men because self-blame is easier for them. "[Women] are especially hard on and judgmental of themselves, before they look to see how others contributed to the problem," observes Dr. John Gray, psychologist. "Men are apt to accuse others before they look at their responsibility for problems."

Indeed, many men apologize only when it's expected or can't be avoided, particularly to avoid fights: "Hey, dude, relax. I said, I'm sorry." Between men, the important issue is status—who's up and who's down. Apologizing puts men in an inferior position, so they tend to avoid it.

Some women, extreme people pleasers, may be overly apologetic because they want to be liked and don't want to make waves. These women say "I'm sorry" for the slightest offense.

Some men disrespect women for being apologetic. Others like it because it shows that women are non-threatening and willing to accept lower status. In *You Just Don't Understand*, Deborah Tannen, Ph.D., writes, "There are many ways that women talk that make sense and are effective in conversations with women, but appear powerless and self-deprecating in conversations with men. One such pattern is that women seem to apologize all the time." As Tannen implies, between women, apologizing is desirable. It keeps women on good terms with one another and encourages intimacy.

Forgive and Forget

It's important to know when and how to apologize. In *Talking Power*, Dr. Robin Lakoff presents rules for apologizing. In order to give an apology, she says, both parties must agree that:

- The apologizer performed the act in question.
- The act was injurious to the receiver of the apology.
- The apologizer needs forgiveness from the hearer.

Each of these facts puts the apologizer in a less powerful position: He or she is in the wrong and must make amends. After that, "The receiver can accept the apology and forgive, or not," says Lakoff. "Apologies are delicate speech arts, and none too popular."

Ritual Apologies

- **In the classroom:** A teacher calls upon a student whose hand is raised, and the student prefaces his/her statement with, "Can I say something?" That's a "ritual apology." Obviously, the student may say something or she/he would not have been called on. The student is afraid of offending others even before anything is said. Female students do this frequently; males rarely.
- **At the office:** You have completed a project at work and you want to show your boss. "Avoid the (mostly female) tendency to apologize, as in `I hope you won't mind looking this over'," writes E. Bingo Wyer in *Cosmopolitan*.

Coping Strategies

- **Women:** Are you overly apologetic? If so, try to apologize less, especially around men. Compare your tone of voice when you apologize to men's. Men's tone is generally less placating and more matter-of-fact.
- **Men:** Don't put women down for being apologetic. This trait works well in their relationships with one another (and probably with you, too). Also, if you rarely apologize, maybe you are overlooking some important opportunities to build rapport.

Advice to Lovers

- Obviously, there is a vast difference between being overly apologetic and saying you're sorry when it's needed. In *Love is Never Enough*, Dr. Aaron T. Beck offers this suggestion: "Don't be afraid to say you're sorry. Loving includes expressing regret when you have unwittingly or deliberately hurt your mate. It is important to communicate this feeling."

♀♂
Laugh Track

Men usually tell more jokes and stories than women

"Did you hear the one about . . . ?" Jokes are attention grabbers. It takes courage to get up in front of others and tell a joke or story. One risks looking foolish or monopolizing the conversation. No wonder many men like to tell them! Being the center of attention is comfortable for them.

My father, Paul, is no exception. He always has at least ten jokes to tell at dinner while I have trouble remembering one. (My sister, Paula, is atypical. She tells great jokes—and she also owns a red Harley Davidson!)

When it comes to personal stories, men's are more likely to have humorous punch lines, but do not tend to be self-deprecating. "Men love a joke—on the other fellow. But your really humorous woman loves a joke on herself," says Mary Roberts Rinehart in *Isn't That Just Like A Man*. Indeed, a study by sociologist Rose Laub Coser, shows that both men and women find it funnier if women are the butt of the joke. "Self-depreciation may be one of the most significant differences between how men and women use humor," says Joe Tanenbaum in *Male & Female Realities*.

His Jokes, Her Jokes
There are gender differences in what is considered funny as well as how jokes are told. In *Women's Folklore, Women's Culture,* Carole Mitchell describes her study on gender and joke-telling. Here are the key findings:

• Men tell a considerably higher percentage than women of overtly hostile and aggressive jokes. Women are more likely to be offended by hostile jokes.

• Men tell more obscene, racial, ethnic, and religious jokes than women do. On the other hand, women exceed men with absurd jokes, morbid jokes, puns, and jokes about authority.

- Women's jokes tend to be shorter then men's.
- Men often enjoy competitive joke-telling sessions, where each man tries to be funnier than the last. Women very rarely do; they worry about hurting others' feelings.
- Men enjoy telling jokes to larger audiences than women. Males prefer an audience of two or more; women prefer one or two.
- Men are more willing to tell jokes to casual acquaintances.
- Both sexes prefer telling jokes to people of the same gender; there is less risk of being misunderstood.
- Men use jokes more aggressively to keep friendships from becoming too intimate. Women attempt to make jokes sound like intimate conversations.
- Men grant prestige to men who have good joke-telling skills. Both men and women think joke-telling is inappropriate for women.

Shtick to the Facts
- Women are more and more claiming humor as legitimate territory. On the nightclub circuit in 1990, women made up 20% of the comics, up from two percent ten years ago, reports *Time*.
- When people were asked by *Psychology Today* whether the wittiest person they knew was a man or a woman, about 83 percent of the males and 68 percent of the females mentioned a man.

For Laughs
- *Women's Glib* (The Crossing Press), a collection of 70 women humorists, edited by Rosalind Warren.
- *Dave Barry's Greatest Hits* (Fawcett).
- *Women in Comedy: Funny Ladies from the Turn of the Century to the Present* (Citadel) by Linda Martin and Kerry Segrave.

♀♂
Help Unwanted

Men are less willing than women to seek assistance from others

Tourists from Maine, Brian and Lori are driving their rental car in Los Angeles. They get lost. Lori says, "There's a gas station. Let's stop right now and get help." Brian doesn't want to stop. He wants to find Disneyland by himself. Lori gets more and more frustrated. "Brian, this driving around is driving me crazy. I want directions now!" After an unproductive fifteen minutes, Brian agrees to stop. At the gas station he says, "You go ask. I'll wait in the car."

As Deborah Tannen and others point out, men often avoid seeking assistance because it's embarrassing and humiliating. It's not manly. Men identify with problem-solving, with being decisive, and being in control. Asking for help puts the person with information in a superior position, while receiving aid makes men feel one-down: "I've failed. I couldn't figure it out myself."

Conversely, women view getting help as a win, like finding an incredible dress at a sale. "Wow, I got the directions. Just what I needed. Fantastic!" Additionally, seeking assistance for women is an opportunity to establish rapport with others. In *The Psychology of Sexual Differences*, Eleanor E. Maccoby and Carol N. Jacklin note, "The female is more likely to ask for help, or to cling to others in the face of threat or challenge, while the male engages in active problem solving."

Given this difference, can you imagine how men feel when they hear, "Honey, I think we should go to a marriage counselor." They would rather ask for directions!

His "Cave Man" Mentality
• "If I'm at a point where I'm angry, I'll ask for directions. The whole thing is a contest: Who will win—me or the

place?. . . Men are like cavemen. They're always working on their hunting skills, trying to be self-sufficient."—Bob Reiss, columnist

• "Why is it that no man can ask for directions? Is it in their DNA or something?" --Jean Gonick, writing in *Glamour*

• "My ancestors wandered lost in the wilderness for 40 years, because even in biblical times, men would not stop and ask for directions."—Elayne Boosler, comedian

Coping Clues

•Women: Respect men's need to be self-sufficient problem solvers. When you want them to seek assistance, expect resistance. You may have to accept the role of the one who does the asking while he waits in the car.

• Men: Respect the ease with which women go for help. Asking for help need not threaten your independence or reflect on your problem-solving skills.

To Go Deeper

• If you'd like to know more about how men really think and feel, read *The Secrets Men Keep* (Ballantine Books) by Dr. Ken Druck with James C. Simmons. Find out about men's deepest fears and fantasies. Find out what's really going on behind the mask of masculinity. The authors say, "No value has gotten modern man into more trouble that than of `being a man.' Traditional lore instructs us from a young age to `grow up and be a man.' Not only is `be a man' as elusive and ambiguous a commandment as has ever been handed down, but we have no idea who originally gave it."

• Another good resource is *Male and Female Realities--Understanding the Opposite Sex* (Robert Erdmann Publishing) by Joe Tanenbaum, an interpersonal communication specialist, corporate trainer, and workshop leader. His terminology is refreshing and original. To order audio tapes, write to: Tanenbaum Associates, 2796 Harbor Blvd., Suite 527, Costa Mesa, CA 92626.

♀♂
Who Boasts Most?

Men tend to boast about their accomplishments more than women

Boasting is competitive, self-focused behavior, and thus is engaged in mostly by men. Men compete by telling others about things that make them look good. Men's successes are public information; they tend to broadcast their accomplishments to whomever will listen: the hole in one, the great speech, the deck he built himself.

Some men are subtle braggarts. They talk around a subject to get other men to guess what they have or have done. Overt braggarts reveal their assets immediately. News anchorperson Bryant Gumble says, "I'm exceedingly self-confident; modestly is not one of my strong suits."

Women's boasting style is more indirect than men's. Most women would rather be liked than admired, applauded, and respected, and prefer telling their successes to intimate friends in private. Additionally, rather than focusing on their accomplishments, women tend to talk about "personal problems" that, from a man's point of view, make them look bad.

It's a Status Display
In *Manwatching*, Desmond Morris says, "Blatant boasting is the typical Status Display of the small boy—`I did it better then you'; No you did not, I did'—but this soon fades with adulthood. It is converted into name-dropping and casually steering conversations boastwards." In other words, as boys grow, boasting still exists, but becomes more subtle. Morris also claims that high-status individuals boast less than low-status types, because they manipulate others into doing it for them by surrounding themselves with flatterers.

She's Modest

• Annabeth Gish, an actress in the movie "Mystic Pizza," was featured in a story for *Mademoiselle* magazine. She said, "When people who don't know you ask, `What did you do last summer?' you don't just drop things like, `Oh, I made a movie.' So you're constantly trying to scope out the situation and figure out how much you can say without bragging." Now that's modesty!

• "Boys like to show off and stuff," said Miranda Canty in the *New York Times*. She's a ten-year-old who has been doing experiments with battery-powered motors at the Girls Inc. program in Lynn, MA. "When it's all girls, they don't show off and say, `I'm better than you.'"

Memos, Memos

To keep your boss abreast of your successes, minor and major, send more memos. Begin them with comments like: "Thought you'd like to know . . . ."

To Explore Further

Many recent books encourage working women to learn the skill of self-promotion, an aspect of assertiveness, to get ahead in business. Here are quotes from two excellent volumes:

• In *Skills for Success* (Ballantine Books), Dr. Adele Scheele, says, "Unlike bragging, which is easy as well as annoying, self-promotion is a subtle skill. And like any skill, it requires a good deal of practice—trail and error—to learn how to make a strong point without coming on *too* strong."

• In *Working With Men* (Beyond Words), Beth Milwid, Ph.D., says "Women strive to be polite, but corporations seek managers that are tough. Women shy from bragging about their accomplishments, but promotions go to those who get the most and the best PR." Given these assumptions, consultants have urged women to mimic men in boasting. But in the past few years, a new trend has emerged. Women are now "intent upon integrating the masculine and the feminine" and are eager to find their way in the business world without becoming like men.

♀♂

When Silence Is Golden

Women tend to nag more than men

Just as boasting is a downside to the self-focused orientation of men, nagging is a potential consequence of women's concentration on others. To nag is to annoy with persistent demands and complaints, and women's urge to nurture can often leads to nagging. Women frequently tell others what to do, for their own good, and when others don't comply, their tone may become pleading, whiny, and angry. "How many times do I have to tell you to . . ."

Indeed, many negative stereotypes of women have grown up around this female tendency. "For most of us, the term *complain* conjures up all sorts of negative images of people who nag, bitch, argue, scream, and otherwise bully others into noticing that they've had it up to here and are not going to take it anymore," says Ellyn Meadors in *New Woman*.

Men's and children's self-directed behaviors often inspire nagging. It's tempting to improve others by urging them to become more considerate, less forgetful, less abusive, and less messy. As mothers, women must socialize their children to be decent, caring human beings, and it's easy, while performing this most difficult of tasks, to fall into nagging. Attempting to change men, however, is condescending—not to mention fruitless (as the enormous popularity of the book *Women Who Love too Much: When You Keep Wishing and Hoping He'll Change* demonstrates).

Many women deny nagging because it's unconscious, and of course not all women do it. And yes, men nag, too, but they do it less, because they care less about how others behave and more about their own performance. Men help perpetuate the nagging cycle, however, by listening to women with one half (or one quarter) of an ear so that women have to repeat their remarks over and over before they sink in.

74

How Nagging Affects Men

• **Ambivalence:** Many men both like and dislike being nagged by women. They like it because it reminds them of their mothers and therefore is associated with attention and love. On the other hand, men don't like listening to complaining or being told what to do. They prefer issuing orders to taking them.

• **Grounds for divorce:** Doris Wild Hemmerling, writer for the *St. Louis Dispatch*, says, "In the last several months, I have watched a number of men decide to leave their marriages, not because of another woman, but because they could no longer endure their wife's negativity. In each case the man thought his wife was a good person and a devoted mother, but he could no longer tolerate living with her."

• **Psychologists' opinion:** "Therapists report that the most common complaint of women in distressed marriages is that their husbands are too withdrawn and don't share openly enough, while the men complain that their wives are overly expressive and emotional to the point of nagging," says Howard Markham, Ph.D., director of the University of Denver's Center for Marital and Family Studies.

• **Different than women:** When nagged by men, most women don't feel as pressured as men do when they are nagged. That's because women's bodies are better at handling stress. "Our [women's] bodies respond to tension with lower surges of stress hormones, and our blood pressure isn't as likely to soar," writes Sue Browder in *Woman*.

Don't Nag, Negotiate!

• If you'd like to nag less and negotiate more, read *Getting to Yes: Negotiating Agreement Without Giving In* (Penguin Books) by Roger Fisher and William Ury. Learn how to establish precise goals.

♀♂
Intimidation Tactics

Men attempt to intimidate others more than women

Football players intimidate opposing team members by sneering, snarling, yelling, cursing, and chest beating. Heads of state bluff and bark at one another. Fathers intimidate sons with insulting language, and sons scowl at their fathers. Big brothers bulldoze over little brothers.

In business, men use intimidation to negotiate deals and move up the corporate ladder. "Tactics of intimidation are directed at rivals on a regular basis in all organizations. In some companies, you have to stand up with your back against the wall because someone is always attacking in order to get one-up on you. It's an all-important fact of life," observes Jay Lorsch, Ph.D., professor of organizational behavior at Harvard University.

Certainly, some women are intimidating. We all know women who come on like Mack trucks. But when the tallies are taken, women intimidators are outnumbered by men. Why? Because women get less intimacy by intimidating. Female traits such as being empathetic, apologetic, approval-seeking, and indirect are not fear-inspiring; they exist to forge bonds, not bulldoze others.

An Unconscious Strategy
Most men don't know how good they are at getting someone to do, or not do, something by inducing fear. Here are a few ways men intimidate lovers and others:

• His silence can be intimidating, "What's he thinking?"

• His direct, decisive mannerisms can be coercive. "He's so blunt."

• His rage can be frightening. "His face becomes moody and hostile. He yells unpredictably and terrifyingly."

• His larger size and superior physical strength can be

alarming. "He looks like Rambo!" (He may even threaten physical violence.)

Stand Up to Intimidators

If you want to feel less intimidated, read a book or take a course on assertiveness. *When I Say No I Feel Guilty* (Bantam Books) by Manuel J. Smith, Ph.D., will help get you started. Here are some of Smith's principles:

• You have the right to change your mind.
• You have the right to make mistakes and take responsibility for them.
• You have the right to be illogical in making decisions.
• You have the right to say "I don't care."
• You have the right to say "I don't know."

Sexual Intimidation

Sexual harassment is a form of bullying. Surveys have shown that 90 percent of Fortune 500 companies have had sexual harassment complaints and nearly 25 percent have been sued repeatedly, reports *Time.* Additionally, surveys have shown that 50 percent of European and 70 percent of Japanese women have been harassed at work. To learn what sexual harassment is and what to do about it, read *Step Forward: Sexual Harassment in the Workplace* (Master-Media) by Susan L. Webb.

Your Own Journey

• **Women:** In the presence of an intimidator, focus more on yourself and less on him (her). If you focus too much on an aggressor, you'll tend to react *fearfully*, which increases their confidence and resolve. Also, anxiety can "interrupt clear thinking, good judgement, adequate problem solving, or appropriate action," warns Karen Johnson, M.D., in *Trusting Ourselves* (Atlantic Monthly Press).
• **Men:** If others shrink, flinch, or crouch in fear when you arrive, perhaps you are coming on too strong. Try to become aware of your intimidating mannerisms and soften your tyrannical tactics. Nobody likes to be bullied.

♀♂

The Right Brothers

Being right is more important to men than women

"I'm right; you're wrong!" Men identify with their decisions and actions more than women do and therefore are very invested in being right. To tell a man what he decided or did was wrong is to strike at his core. It suggests that he has lost respect as an authority and since he is self-focused, his authority is what he must rely on to navigate in the world. "Men always have to be right," says Dr. John Gray in *Men, Women And Relationships*.

Remember that men talk more about things and less about people? Well, having the right answers is one area where men want to be right. The foundation of many men's conversations, especially with one another, is largely based on numbers, how things work, which model is best and so on. If you put down their knowledge, you put men down.

Most women care less about defending their decisions, actions, and facts. They may argue with you, but they have less invested in being experts. Often in arguments, what they are looking for is a validation of their emotions, not proof that one or the other side is correct: "I think it's not safe for Johnny to go to the concert alone. I would be afraid the whole time. Don't you agree?" Men, on the other hand, are much more concerned with pinning the facts down: "The truth is that only three teenage boys in the past year have been abducted from the streets in the U.S. Odds are he'll be fine." This can make for extremely frustrating conversations for both sexes.

Quotable Quotes
• "One of the hardest lessons to learn in marriage is to let your partner have his or her own opinions and ways of doing things. We are conditioned to think that our way is

the right way." —Lee Johnson-Kaufman, columnist
• "Would you rather be right or happy? A lot of people argue about who's right. The right way to roll socks. The right way to open a can." —Jennifer James, Ph.D. psychologist

Male Answer Syndrome
Humorist Jane Campbell, writing in *Details*, has identified a strange disorder rampant among men that she calls Male Answer Syndrome—"the chronic answering of questions regardless of actual knowledge . . . The compulsion to answer varies from person to person, but few men are happy saying 'I don't know.' They prefer 'That's not what's important here.'" The syndrome can be dangerous, she claims. "Men can speak with such conviction that women may be fooled into thinking that they actually know what they're talking about."

How to Cope
Here are some tips for dealing with people who make you wrong:
• If you get caught in a petty debate, switch sides in midstream. "You know, that's a good point . . . " Why argue over trivialities?
• Always consider the source when someone tells you that you are wrong. Often, a response isn't even deserved.
• Play devil's advocate judiciously. Most men, and many women, have a lot of ego invested in what they say and do. Think before you strike.

A Spiritual Approach
• Read *The Art of Living: Vipassana Meditation* (Harper & Row) as taught by S.N. Goenka who says, "We fail to recognize that each person has his or her own beliefs. It is futile to argue over which view is correct; more beneficial would be to set aside any preconceived notions and to try to see reality."

♀♂
May I Take Your Order?

Men generally feel more comfortable giving orders than women do

"Don't tell me what to do!" Most men would rather give orders than take them. In a man's world, the person giving the orders is seen as superior and the receiver is seen as inferior. Men actively seek the superior position. In *Talking Power*, Robin Lakoff says, "To utter a direct order is not kind or gentle, since it makes it brutally obvious that the speaker outranks, and has power to control the actions of, the hearer."

To get someone to do something, you can appeal to them by commanding, demanding, requesting, or suggesting. Commands and demands are powerful, purposeful, and militaristic. Suggestions and requests are softer and easier to dismiss.

Women's orders tend to sound like suggestions. They are often prefaced with niceties like: "Would you mind if we..." or "If it's not too much trouble, could you...?" According to linguist Deborah Tannen, "Girls don't give orders; they express their preferences as suggestions... Whereas boys say, `Gimme that!' and `Get outta here!,' girls say 'Let's do this' and 'How about doing that?'" Since women are particularly concerned with the feelings of others, they are uncomfortable with direct orders that can wound the ego of the other person.

Women in Business
In the business world, many successful career women have learned to issue orders effectively. And some have learned that they would rather issue orders in their own softer way. "In record numbers, some of America's most talented women are leaving mainstream institutions to create institutions of their own. One reason for this trend is their

collective disdain for a world dominated by power, ego, and competition. An equally compelling reason is their sense that access to the top is virtually cut off," writes Beth Milwid in *Working With Men.*

Boys & Girls
Looking at boys' and girls' behavior may give us clues as to why it's easier for men to issue orders than women. Here are two quotes from Maccoby's and Jacklin's book, *The Psychology of Sex Differences:*
• **Dominance:** "Dominance appears to be more of an issue with boys' groups than girls' groups. Boys make more dominance attempts (both successful and unsuccessful) toward one another than girls do. They also more often attempt to dominate adults."
• **Compliance:** "In childhood, girls tend to be more compliant to the demands and directions of adults. This compliance doesn't extend to willingness to accept directions from, or be influenced by, age-mates."

One-up, One-Down
If you'd like to give orders so both the speaker and the addressee feel comfortable, here are four ways to do it. These suggestions are especially useful on the home front, but can be very effective at work as well.
• **Phrase orders as questions.** "Could you wash the car on Saturday?"
• **Preface orders with compliments.** "You look strong enough to bring in the firewood."
• **Preface orders with "please."** This word takes the edge off. "Please be sure to do the laundry."
• **Allow the person to do it within his or her own time frame.** "Please rake the leaves sometime between now and Friday." This acknowledges that the other person has her own preferences and desires, and that you trust her to do the job without standing over her.

♀♂
Clearing the Air

Women tend to be less confrontational than men

Men like conflict. They relish power struggles in business, sports, and personal relationships. Women tend to avoid conflict and take it more seriously than men. After a fight, a woman may feel terrible—sometimes for several days. A man may feel better for having the fight and usually is able to "not take it personally."

Women tend to avoid confrontations. "We [women] are anxious about pleasing other people, so we hesitate to speak up about what we think or feel. We qualify our statements with phrases like `I kinda think' or `I sorta feel,'" write the members of the Seattle-King NOW Chapter in their book, *Women, Assert Yourself!*

At work, men are more apt to confront the boss than women. "Men are naturally competitive with anyone in authority," writes Lynn Darling in *Self.* "Women are intimidated by it. They don't understand the game. Women don't challenge because they fear crossing the line. If they have a big fight, they think they have to quit (their job). Men think they will have to have another fight."

Male Fighting Style
David McDonough, writing in *Men's Health*, identifies one aspect of men's fighting technique that infuriates women—"the device we call *feudus interruptus*. This refers to the astonishing ability men have to engage in verbal combat with all the venom of a rattlesnake, suspend the argument for a four-hour period while we are out with friends, be charming and outgoing . . . as if nothing had happened. . . [then] pick up the argument at the exact point where we left off."

Quotable Quotes

• "Conflict has been a taboo area for women and for key reasons. Women are supposed to be the quintessential accommodators, mediators, the adapters, and the soothers. Yet conflict is necessary if women are to build for the future." —Jean Baker Miller, *Toward a New Psychology for Women*

• "For the truly loving person the act of criticism or confrontation doesn't come easily; to such a person it is evident that the act has great potential for arrogance." —M. Scott Peck, M.D., *The Road Less Traveled*

• "Conflict can identify problems, help define who we are, and discharge some resentments." —James Creighton, *Don't Go Away Mad*

To Go Deeper

Conflict doesn't have to be a negative form of communication. If you fight with a particular goal in mind, and fight fair, conflict can lead to better understanding. For suggestions on how to handle conflict, read *Love is Never Enough* (Perennial Library) by Aaron T. Beck, M.D. Here are a few of his tips for constructive conflict:

• Be brief: Focus on one issue only. Stick to the point.

• Be specific: Instead of saying, "I'd like you to be neater," say, "I'd like you to put your clothes in the laundry basket."

• Avoid insulting labels: Don't tell someone she is a "slob" or "lazy."

• Avoid absolutes: Don't tell someone he *always* or *never* does it a certain way. It's never true.

• State problems positively: Say, "It would be great if you'd help with the housework," rather than "You *don't* help with the housework."

• Don't analyze another person's motives: This is upsetting—and you may be wrong.

• Call "time-out" if the conflict becomes too heated. Resume it another day.

THE SCOOP
ON ROMANCE

♀♂

To Marry or Tarry

Men tend to fear commitment
more than women

Much has been written about men's fear of commitment. According to the Hite Report, 82 percent of single women say that most men they know want to avoid commitments. A relationship in which one party wants a commitment and the other doesn't is unequal—the uncommitted person is one-up and the committed person is one-down. More men than women have the upper hand in these unequal relationships.

Women fear commitment, too, but much less than men. "Even though a woman may fear commitment, she has many other fears, needs and instincts that are continually urging her to commit," says Stephen Carter in *Men Who Can't Love.*

Reasons for Reluctance
• "If she quits work to have children, I'll be responsible for all of the expenses." Men view marriage as a major economic responsibility.
• "If we spend more time together, I'll feel smothered." Men need to control distance with others, so they will not feel engulfed, and marriage with its daily domestic component threatens distance.
• "What if I meet someone I like better!" Men suffer from the Grass Is Greener Syndrome more than women and fear making a choice they'll regret later.
• "I can take care of myself." Psychologist Warren Farrell says, "Now men feel less as if they have to marry for sex; they are aware that housework can be hired out and that restaurants serve meals; they are less trapped by the family-man image."
• "I'm afraid we'll end up getting a divorce." Today many

people of both genders are wary of marriage because 50 percent end in divorce.

Stall Tactics
Men, more than women, find themselves in ambivalent relationships. They don't want to marry *or* give up their lover. So when the subject of marriage comes up, they stall; change the subject abruptly; talk about marriage in a cynical way; dwell on the failures of mutual friends; agree to talk about marriage only after they get a promotion or better job—"In six months I'll find out if I get promoted to that position in L.A., then we can talk about us."; or engage in Future Talk: "After we get married, we'll buy a ski cabin at Tahoe." This tactic tricks some women into thinking they have a commitment when, in fact, they don't.

When He Marries, Finally!
What do men look for in a mate? According to studies done by psychologist Douglas Kendrick of Arizona State University, "Men show a strong preference for physical attractiveness when evaluating potential mates, while women pay more attention to a man's social status and material resources," writes Bruce Bower in *Science News*.

Marriage Healthy for Men
Scientists at the UC San Francisco found that unmarried men are particularly vulnerable to early death. Of men aged 45 to 54 who were unmarried, 23 percent died within ten years, compared to 11 percent of their married peers. Marriage confers longevity on women as well, but not as dramatically. "This is probably true to the extent that (marriage) saves (men) from the terrible isolation and lack of intimacy that characterizes masculinity," says Herb Goldberg, psychologist.

A Starting Point
• If you're in love with a noncommitter, read *Cold Feet— Why Men Don't Commit* (New American Library) by Dr. Sonya Rhodes and Dr. Marlin S. Potash.

♀♂

Lovaholics Anonymous

Women more than men can become "addicted" to a love relationship

Everyone wants to love and be loved. But often women can more easily lose themselves in love, becoming overly dependent and needy, suffering great pain when a lover is unavailable, emotionally or physically, literally feeling that "I can't live without him."

There has been a great deal of attention on this recently in the media and some psychologists have gone so far as to consider it an addiction, perhaps even with a physical component. "It has been found that people in the first flush of falling in love generate large quantities of arousing brain drugs such as phenylethylamine, dopamine, and norepinephrine. In proper combination, these brain drugs have an effect like cocaine," says Michael Hutchison in *The Anatomy of Sex and Power.*

Love-addicted women are *heavily* other-focused and have low self-esteem. They readily give up what sense of self they have to submerge themselves into a lover. Psychologist Robin Norwood notes, "It is familiar and comforting to many women who love too much to feel that they are taking care of (managing and controlling) another person."

Men worship their lovers less frequently than women do. They're more apt to be attention-getters than givers. Their stronger sense of self doesn't allow them to be consumed by another person. (On the other hand, worshipped men are usually *heavily* self-focused, and despite the adulation they inspire, they have low self-esteem and need someone to constantly build their egos.)

Dyan and Cary
Some women's emotions are triggered more by loving

than being loved. For example, Dyan Cannon *adored* her husband Cary Grant. He was famous, handsome, intelligent, and witty. Her life revolved around him, and she did everything possible to be a perfect wife. Years after her divorce Dyan revealed, "I had been with Cary about four years, never saw another man, and really loved him—which means that I adored him, I revered him, he was like God. But none of those things a happy marriage make."

Commendable Comments

• "We *speak* of the distinctions between healthy love and addictive love, but in our deepest hearts, we really believe there is only one kind of true love—and that unless we are obsessed, in the grip of a physical dependency, we are not truly in love—but only in *like*" —Erica Jong, *Any Woman's Blues*

• "Addiction is discontinued when a person possesses a tangible sense of freedom and self-command—a sense of having power to fashion the conditions of his or her life instead of being fashioned by them." —Dr. Stanton Peele, *Love and Addiction*

To Go Deeper

Loving focuses on others; being loved focuses on the self. A balance of both creates healthy relationships.

• If you are in an addictive relationship, read the classic, *Women Who Love Too Much* (Pocket Books) by Robin Norwood. Through a series of case histories, and a ten-point recovery program, Norwood offers a way to become free of destructive loving.

• *Smart Love* (Jeremy P. Tarcher, Inc.) by Jody Hayes, San Francisco based writer and lecturer. This is a workbook which shows readers how to let go of painful patterns and obsessions with others.

• *Love and Addiction* (New American Library) by Stanton Peele. Learn why we often say "love" when we are acting out an addiction.

♀♂
Losing a Lover

Women are emotionally jealous; men are sexually jealous

"What matters in a relationship is not whether jealousy is present, but to what degree it exists," writes Shelley Levitt in *New Woman*. The fear of losing a lover to another disturbs both men and women. How and when they feel it and express it is very different.

When men succumb to jealous emotions, watch out! "Researchers have found that in all cultures male jealousy constitutes the leading cause of spousal homicide, and is also the cause of most wife-beating as well," writes Michael Hutchison in *The Anatomy of Sex and Power*. Implicit in such male jealousy is the idea that a woman somehow belongs to a man and men are fearful of losing that control. Dr. Allan Pass, psychologist, explains: "An obsessively jealous male usually views the woman as a possession. He is selfish, very narcissistic. He believes that the woman must do everything he wants her to do."

Female jealousy tends to be expressed verbally by crying, pleading, accusing—"I saw the way you looked at Shannon"—and is motivated by much more overt insecurity. Because women value their relationships so highly and identify with them so strongly, they are fearful of losing their connection. Women also tend to express their jealousy more, leading many people to consider them more jealous.

When Threatened with a Rival ...

• **Her jealousy is over "emotional infidelity":** According to psychologist David M. Buss of the University of Michigan, female jealousy revolves around the loss of emotional commitment.

• **His jealousy focuses on "sexual infidelity":** "Maybe another man fathered my child?" (Women don't have such

90

worries.) Also, it's humiliating for a man to lose out to an interloper, because in the jealous man's mind, he is one-down and the other man is one-up. Status is at stake.

Reasons for Jealousy

Everybody gets jealous now and then, because "the loss of a lover is a primal human fear," writes Katherine Merlin in *Cosmopolitan*. People become jealous for a variety of reasons. They may overreact to an innocent encounter between their lover and another person. Or sense a real threat to their relationship. They may love someone who is inherently unfaithful. Or jealousy may simply remind them of how much they care about their mate.

Fascinating Findings

In a *Psychology Today* article, "Getting at the Heart of Jealous Love," Virginia Adams cites the results of several studies that offer the following:

• When a relationship is threatened by an outsider, women often react by trying to save the relationship, while men focus on saving face.

• For women, feelings of inadequacy often lead to jealousy, while men get feelings of inadequacy *after* they have a concrete reason to be jealous.

• The less education people have, the more jealous they are.

• Younger people are more jealous than older people, and long-time relationships have fewer jealous feelings than newer ones.

• Women react more intensely than men when asked how jealous they would feel if a mate was unfaithful.

• Men are more apt to blame their jealousy on others, whereas women tend to blame themselves.

To Explore Further

• *The Green-Eyed Marriage: Surviving Jealous Relationships* (The Free Press) by Dr. Robert L. Barker, a marital therapist, offers real help to men and women who suffer because of jealousy.

♀♂

Hooked on Hope

Women more than men try to change others

"It's a miracle we've met. You're everything I want to change in a man." More than men, women spend time and energy trying to change their mates. "Maybe the real difference between men and women is that men understand the difference and accept it, whereas women don't understand it and want men to change," says Michael E. McGill, Ph.D., psychologist.

What motivates women to change others? Optimism? Self-righteousness? A belief that love conquers all? That frogs turn into princes? Women become reformers—hope addicts—because they feel responsible for others, want to be needed, want to be treated better, want to feel closer to others. All good reasons. But people don't usually change for others; they change when they are ready—or inspired! And unfortunately, focusing on changing others often gets in the way of dumping a loser, improving oneself, or accepting others as they are.

By contrast, men tend to take their spouses as they are, thinking, "What you see is what you get!" Men look at the numbers—"What are the odds of changing him/her?"—and conclude, "Not good." Men would rather solve concrete problems. Trying to change others is like swimming against the current. Men go with the flow not only because it's less stressful, but because they are most concerned with themselves, not others. Therefore they have no real interest in converting anyone else.

Many women *resent* men's self-focused behaviors and try to remake men into creatures like themselves. Many men, on the other hand, rather than attempting to change women, become *disrespectful* and annoyed.

Words to the Wise
• Trying to change others is usually frustrating. In *Love*

Against Hate, Dr. Karl Menninger writes about women who rescue men: "She appeals to him because she is a rescuer; he appeals to her because she needs someone to save. When after a period of success, her efforts fail, as they are likely to do, she is overwhelmed with a feeling of defeat."

• In *Secrets About Men Every Women Should Know,* Barbara DeAngelis, Ph.D., gives this advice to hope-addicts: "Having a healthy relationship with a man means loving him for who he is *now,* and not loving him *in spite of* who he is today, or *in hopes* of who he will be tomorrow."

• Sonya Friedman, in her book *Men are Just Desserts,* writes, "If you seek out a man in need of rehabilitation, you may well discover you're in for a bumpy ride."

In the Genes?

• **The Twin Study:** In a landmark study of twins raised apart, University of Minnesota researchers found that between 50 percent and 70 percent of personality traits are determined by heredity. Dr. David T. Lykken, one of the study's authors, says, "The environment molds your personality, but your genes determine what kind of environment you seek." You can't change genes.

How to Criticize

Suppose he's chronically late, messy, or eats like a pig. Here are some of *Mademoiselle* writer Dalma Heyn's guidelines for changing men:

• Only criticize that which hurts or annoys you most.
• Be precise about what it is you want him to change.
• Don't attack his character.
• Use wit and style to help him effect the change you're requesting.

To Go Deeper

• *Do I Have To Give Up Me to be Loved By You?* (CompCare) by Jordan Paul and Margaret Paul.
• To learn more about how to love and be loved, read *True Love: How to Make Your Relationship Sweeter, Deeper and More Passionate* (Conari Press) by Daphne Rose Kingma. It's a little gem of a book.

♀♂

Givers & Takers

Women tend to give more than men

For women, giving is like breathing—it's sustenance. Women tend to give a lot because they focus on others; being nurturing is a strongly-held female value. In fact, it is so much a part of who women are that they can go overboard. In *Gift From The Sea*, Anne Morrow Lindbergh says, "Traditionally, we [women] are taught, and instinctively we long, to give where it is needed—and immediately. Eternally, woman spills herself away in driplets to the thirsty."

Men on the other hand, give more cautiously and are more conscious of what they will get in return. "The question of whether he is a giver or giving enough doesn't enter into a man's self-image. Few men feel that giving is a primary issue in their struggles for identity. They are concerned much more about 'doing.' Am I a doer?'," explains Jean Baker Miller, M.D., in *Toward a New Psychology of Women*.

Morton Shaevitz, Ph.D., describes men this way: "It is not yet clear whether the source of the lack of nurturing is biological or learned, but men tend to nurture less. They are not as spontaneously giving. They don't naturally care for, or take care of, others. This is true at home and in the workplace."

It's Really about *Focus*

As many women have been learning in their journey of self discovery, it's not better to give then to receive. It's best to do both in equal proportion. Giving and receiving is primarily about *focus*—to truly give, focus on another. To truly receive, focus on yourself.

• **Women's focus:** Many women have trouble emotionally receiving because they don't focus enough on themselves. An example: A man gives a woman a dozen roses, and she

doesn't really receive them, because her attention is primarily on him. Consequently, she doesn't truly take in the message they are conveying: I love you; you are important to me. The roses are put in a vase and she says, "Oh, they're lovely!" but she hasn't allowed herself to feel the meaning.
• **Man's focus:** Many men don't truly give because they don't focus enough on others while giving. Psychologist Michael E. McGill says, "Men use gifts as vehicles for expressing their feelings. Whatever the means and meaning, a particular man may attach to his gifting, women are quick to point out a common pattern in a man's presents; he rarely gives of himself."

Intrusive Giving

• "Sometimes we must not give, for to give would be to intrude. And sometimes—when we are lucky, when we are blessed—we are permitted to share what we have."
—John-Roger and Peter McWilliams, *Life 101*
• "The motives behind injudicious giving and destructive nourishing are many, but such cases invariably have a basic feature in common: the `giver,' under the guise of love, is responding to and meeting his or her own needs without regard to the spiritual needs of the receiver."
—M. Scott Peck, *The Road Less Traveled*

Your Own Journey

• Read *The Givers and the Takers* (Fawcett) by Cris Evatt and Bruce Feld. One psychologist called this "the first book on codependency." Here are some of its remedies:
   1. Give to the givers, and take from the takers;
   2. Become familiar with taker tricks, designed to get things;
   3. Become familiar with giver tricks, designed to avoid receiving things;
   4. Be wary of taker guilt and giver resentment;
   5. Givers and takers can learn from each other.

♀♂
Three's a Crowd

Men tend to be more polygamous than women

Women tend to crave monogamy and men, even if they personally do not stray, tend to place less value on fidelity. Why?

Genetics may be one reason. "Male promiscuity has an evolutionary pedigree. It made sense to add to the number of the tribe at every opportunity. The greater the number of offspring, the greater the chance of passing on his genes to the next generation," writes Anne Moir in *Brain Sex*. "Promiscuity is encoded in the male genes and imprinted on the male brain's circuitboard."

However, today's women don't want Stone Age men. They want faithful lovers—and when their lovers are polygamous, they suffer. Obviously, not all men are unfaithful. Many are loyal companions who won't risk losing their lover either for a short fling or long affair.

However, men do stray more. Just how much is unclear. Statistical figures vary widely—the 1990 Kinsey Report says 37 percent of men and 29 percent of women are unfaithful while a University of Chicago survey claims 70 percent of men and 30 percent of women have had affairs. One of the problems with such research, notes Susan Barbieri of the *Orlando Sentinel*, is that it "depends on truthful answers, and infidelity depends on deceit."

Why Stray?
According to a survey in *USA Today*, many women who are unfaithful stray because their spouse is aloof and preoccupied with work: "I wanted more affection and companionship and love." Both women and men cite boring sex, or no sex, as a reason for an affair.

Love Triangles
"Three people love him—I love him, she loves him, and he

loves himself." So complain women caught in love triangles with another woman and a man. The man, of course, relishes being the center of attention. If the women know about each other, they tend to be hopeful, "He'll probably dump her, not me." Some men will string two women along until one takes a stand. "I'm upfront with both of them. It's their responsibility to break up with me if they don't like the situation. If I had my way, I'd like them to be *friends*." (I actually heard a man say that—on Oprah, no less.) Women play this game far less frequently.

Extramarital Facts of Life
• "Monogamy is rare in mammals, almost unheard of in primates, and it appears to be a relatively recent invention of certain human cultures." —David Barash, zoologist
• "Of 116 societies in a cross-cultural study, 65 percent were more tolerant of adultery by men than by women; none was more tolerant of adultery by women." —Michael Hutchison, *The Anatomy of Sex and Power*.
• According to *Do You Do it With the Lights On?*, 51% of men fantasize about someone else during sex, while only 37% of women do.

He Says, She Says
• **Sylvester Stallone:** "Men sometimes wander for mindless reasons. It has nothing to do with hurting their wives, but the damage to their relationship is irreparable anyway."
• **Dr. Joyce Brothers:** "A wife's infidelity poses a greater threat to the marriage than a husband's. Men react with anger, jealousy, and sometimes physical violence when they learn that their wife has been unfaithful.... The man's ego is far more damaged than that of the woman who discovers that her husband has betrayed her."

To Explore Further
• In *Secret Lovers: Affairs Happen ... How To Cope* (Lexington Books), Dr. Luann Linquist breaks through myths about affairs to show what is really happening.

♀♂

Dysfunctional Dynamics

In dysfunctional relationships, women tend to be masochistic and men tend to be sadistic

"He beats me." "Why don't you leave?" "I can't." Many women come to therapy with an anthology of abuse stories. According to the Bureau of Justice, over 50 percent of all women will experience violence in an intimate relationship and for 24-30 percent, the battering will be regular and ongoing.

Abused women can often clearly describe their predicament and yet, at the same time, readily forgive their abusers. Such women are extremely other-focused, passive, and masochistic. In the past, the word "masochistic" was used strictly in sexual contexts. Now it's used more broadly to include people who tolerate abuse of any kind. Writer Erica Jong says, "How many successful women have lingered for years in debilitating relationships, fueled by masochism and substance abuse? How many women feed the hand that bites them? Men do this too, of course—but with women it seems a plague."

Women stay in abusive relationships for many reasons: They may be financially dependent. They may fear making changes. They may fear raising their children alone. Perhaps they don't think it's possible to be in a relationship that is free of suffering, because abuse is commonplace in their personal histories. They may think that violence is an appropriate response to their behavior. It's not. It's the responsibility of the violent person.

Portrait of an Abuser

Many batterers have Dr. Jekyll/Mr. Hyde personalities. They're like two different people—nice one minute, and cruel the next. "The batterer can be either very, very good or very, very horrid. Furthermore, he can swing back and

98

forth between the two characters with the smoothness of the con artist. But unlike the psychopath, the batterer feels a sense of guilt and shame at his uncontrollable actions. If he were able to cease the violence, he would," says Lenore E. Walker in *The Battered Woman*.

The "Men Are Superior" Myth

Why men are abusive is complicated. "Research indicates somewhere around 60 percent of men who batter grew up in homes where they were beaten or witnessed one parent battering another. But what about the other 40 percent?" says the National Coalition Against Domestic Violence.

In many cases, the "batterer believes that when it comes to his wife, he's accountable to no one. Consciously or not, he has bought into the attitude that men are superior to women, and that `his' woman is there to obey him and respond to his needs. He sees violence as an acceptable tool for enforcing his authority," writes Joy Zimmerman in the *Pacific Sun*.

Facing the Facts

• Every 15 seconds the crime of battering occurs in the United States.

• Up to 35 percent of emergency room visits by women are for abuse-related injuries, reports the *Journal of the American Medical Association*.

• Alcohol is involved in up to 80 percent of all reported spouse abuse, according to *The Recovery Resource Book*.

A Starting Point

• For more information, write to The National Coalition Against Domestic Violence; P.O. Box 34103; Washington, D.C. 20043-4103, (202) 638-6388.

• If you're being abused, get out! Study after study shows it will not stop without outside intervention no matter what you do. Most communities now have some kind of shelters for battered women. Look in the Yellow Pages or call your local women's center.

♀♂
Getting Off on Sex

Men tend to want more sex
and women want more love in relationships

Remember the great scene in "Annie Hall" where they answer the therapist's question, "How often do you have sex?" She says, "Constantly, three times a week." He says, "Hardly ever, three times a week." The problem isn't just in the movies. A 1988 survey of 289 sex therapists found that the number one complaint among couples was a discrepancy in sexual desire, with men wanting sex more often than women. And a survey by *Longevity Magazine* found that about 70 percent of men as compared to 54 percent of women would like to make love more than three times a week.

It is commonly believed that men view sex as a physical release, a diversion, more than women. "For men, the desire for sexual activity is like an itch that grows in intensity and needs to be scratched; for women, sexual desire is muted and needs to be piqued," writes Paula M. Siegel in *Self*.

Wanting more sex is usually a male issue, while wanting more love—affection, closeness—tends to be a female desire. "Women want to feel love before having sex and men feel more closeness as a result of sex," says Diane Kramer in *Why Men Don't Get Enough Sex and Women Don't Get Enough Love*.

Additionally, men, more than women, are concerned with sexual performance: Did I give her an orgasm? Did I last long enough? In *Male Sexuality*, Bernie Zilbergeld says, "Men have been duped. They have accepted unrealistic and, in fact, superhuman standards by which to measure their equipment, performance and satisfaction."

The Difference that Makes the Difference
• "The limited exposure women have to testosterone oc-

curs mainly at puberty, when they begin to manufacture their own. Males manufacture significant levels of it while in the uterus as well as during and after adolescence. We suspect that early exposure to testosterone makes the brain more responsive to the hormone later on, producing a stronger, more persistent sex drive," says Patricia Schreiner-Engel, Ph.D., at Mount Sinai School of Medicine, New York City.

The Sexperts

• **Dr. Ruth Westheimer:** "It is common for couples to experience different levels of desire." Dr. Ruth suggests that occasionally men should give women the hugging and kissing they desire, and women should give men the sexual pleasure they desire "even when you don't." She believes that "compromise is the key when sex drives differ."

• **Harry Stein, editor:** "The difference between the male and female sex drive is apt to be the difference between shooting a bullet and throwing one."

Sex Facts

According to *Self* magazine:

• After making love, it takes a man about 30 minutes to become aroused again; women can become aroused again immediately.

• Men reach their sexual peak by age 20 and women by age 35.

• Men are more apt to misinterpret a woman's friendliness as a sign of sexual availability.

To Go Deeper

• *Woman's Experience of Sex: The Facts and Feelings of Female Sexuality at Every Stage of Life* (Penguin Books) by Sheila Kitzinger.

• *Male Sexuality* (Bantam) by Bernie Zilbergeld, Ph.D.

• *Do You Do It with the Lights On?* (Fawcett) by Mel Poretz and Barry Sinrod is a fascinating compendium of sex secrets and statistics.

FRIENDS
& FOES

Getting Friendly

Women tend to have more intimate friends than men do

There's an old saying: "Men make better fishing buddies, but women make better friends." Close relationships are women's lifeblood. Their friendships tend to be more intimate, intense, and demonstrative than men's. They are easily affectionate to friends, and readily share personal thoughts and feelings that men tend to hold back. "When I asked women if they had a best friend, they nearly always had an affirmative answer, but when I asked men, the question was often met with a kind of silence," says Dr. Lillian Rubin in *Just Friends*.

Sharing vulnerabilities brings people closer together. But since men's relationships tend to be based on competition, revealing weaknesses can be seen as self-defeating. Many men think, "If I tell another man my personal problems, he might use them against me." Men tend to be distrustful, impersonal, and less demonstrative with other men. Protecting their own egos is foremost. "I use the phrase `moments of intimacy' as a way to describe what generally occurs between men. Openness about feelings takes place rarely and under very special circumstances," says psychologist Morton Shaevitz.

Then there's homophobia. Some men actually fear being considered gay if they reveal their feelings to other men. Writer Perry Garfinkel says, "Homophobia accounts for one of the major barriers inhibiting closer and more intimate relationships between men .... The fear of it—in others, in themselves—makes them think twice about touching each other with any more tenderness than that displayed in beefy bearhugs or quick pats on the shoulder. It makes men avert their eyes from a stare held too long."

In *The Male Machine*, Marc Fasteau sums it up: "Despite the time men spend together, their contact rarely goes beyond the external, a limitation which tends to make their friendships shallow and unsatisfying."

Man's Best Friend
You've heard that a dog is man's best friend. Not so! According to a *Men's Life* survey, 90 percent of married men say their wives are their best friends. In *Women's Reality*, Anne Wilson Schaef concurs, "Many of the men I see in therapy tell me that they have no one with whom they really share themselves except for their wives. The wives, on the other hand, almost always have at least one close woman friend."

Friendship Fact
A study done at UCLA found that elderly men, when dealing with the death of a close family member other than a spouse, suffer much greater depression than women. Researcher Judith M. Siegel, Ph.D., speculates the reason is because men have fewer close friends to turn to.

Changes on the Horizon?
Boys who aren't pushed to be tough and self-reliant are just as likely as girls to forge close friendships, according to a new study reported in *American Health*. USC researchers found that boys who are "sensitive but not sissies, with a healthy quota of both masculine and feminine traits" trust and feel closer to male friends than "macho" boys. Says researcher Dr. Gerald Jones, "To encourage your son's friendly side, praise him when he shows an interest in other people's feelings."

Further Resources
• *Men & Friendship* (Gateway Books) by Stuart Miller is based on nearly a thousand interviews with men. This book invites men to find ways to overcome barriers to real friendship.
• *Just Friends: The Role of Friendship in Our Lives* (Harper & Row) by Dr. Lillian Rubin.

Members of the Pack

Men like group activities more than women

"Let's get together with the guys!" Football on television, basketball at a local park, volleyball on the beach, fishing and hunting trips, mountain treks in uncharted territories, motorcycle gatherings in Montana, car cruising on the main drag, and drinking at a pub are just a few activities that bring men together. Writing in *Self*, Dan Zevin asks, "Why do men have to go somewhere or do something when they get together? Why can't they just sit down and talk, the way women do?" Because men are less verbal!

Joining with other men in an activity, or to talk about doing something, is the middle road between isolation and intimacy that many men like—just think of fraternities, secret societies, and men's clubs. Camaraderie between men even has a name, "male bonding," a phrase coined by Rutgers University anthropologist Lionel Tiger in the late sixties. Tiger says male bonding is a process with biological roots that has been going on since prehistoric times "when men formed hunting and gathering packs so they could defend their communities." Men who were willing and able to bond dominated those who didn't and therefore, over time, had a genetic advantage.

Males, says Tiger, bond in a variety of situations involving power, force and dangerous work, and "consciously and emotionally exclude females from these bonds." (The *Unofficial College Dictionary* defines a "male bonding event" as "What you call a party when no girls show up.")

Generally speaking, women prefer one-to-one encounters (or a small intimate group) to large group activities. When women get together, it's usually to talk—just think of coffee klatsches and slumber parties. Women tell secrets, share feelings, and air personal problems.

Gathering of Tribes

The newest male bonding rituals are being offered by the men's movement in a potpourri of conferences, retreats and weekly groups. Typically there's drumming, dancing, howling, chanting, sitting in sweat lodges, and storytelling as men begin to relate to one another in nontraditional ways. Will these groups replace more traditional forms of male bonding? Only time will tell.

Boys & Girls at Play

Stanford University researchers Eleanor Maccoby and Carol Jacklin have extensively studied groups of boys and groups of girls playing together. Here's some of what they found:

- Both sexes prefer same-sex playmates.
- Girls feel uncomfortable around boys' rough-and-tumble style and find it difficult to influence boys.
- Boys in groups tend to cut-up and fool around more, while girls tend to be more serious.
- Boys more than girls, are concerned with dominance and competition.
- Boys interrupt each other more often and call one another names more.
- Girls, in all-girl groups, express agreement with one another more often.
- Girls pause to give one another a chance to speak; boys use speech to protect turf and banter for status.
- Boys' groups are more hierarchical than girls'.

To Go Deeper

- *Men in Groups* (Marion Boyars) by Lionel Tiger is an excellent resource on male bonding.
- *In a Man's World* (Signet) by Perry Garfinkel will give you the low-down on men's clubs, fathers and sons, and male friendships. "As a man moves through life, he becomes a member of many men's clubs, organizations, and fraternities. They exist in all social strata—from the Harvard Club to the Harlem playground," explains Garfinkel.

♀♂

The Trust Busters

Men trust others less than women do

"I don't trust him." Men have trouble trusting other men because of the competitive nature of their relationships. Since each man proves himself by measuring his performance against other men's, it's easy for men to feel that they can only trust themselves. Perry Garfinkel, the author of *In a Man's World*, says "In a competitive environment, there are few men you can trust. That lesson has been brought home for men."

"For trust to develop, there must be disclosures; for disclosures, there must be trust," says psychologist Michael McGill. Too often men guard their innermost thoughts and feelings from others. This habit leads to suspicion, for how can you trust someone you don't know well?

Men do tend to trust women. In *The Secrets Men Keep*, psychologist Ken Druck says, "Men feel safer talking to a woman about their fears and uncertainties than to another man. We [men] perceive women as more loving and trustworthy than other men."

Women, with their less competitive tendencies and stronger ability to share feelings, have much fewer problems with trust. Indeed, trust is an important factor in their relationships. It helps them to get what they want—intimacy, approval, and love. Women instinctively know that trust nurtures, and distrust undermines closeness. Consequently, women aren't as good at deceiving others. In her book *The Opposite Sex*, Dr. Anne Campbell writes, "Women's openness is also reflected in the fact that they do not excel at deceit: when asked to suppress an emotion, women `leak' their true feelings to a greater extent than men."

Women More Gullible?
"How could she fall for those lines?" Some women trust too much. They are easily duped, dazzled, and cheated. Dr.

Anne Campbell says, "While women may be more successful than men at reading other people's undisguised emotions, they do not spot deceptions as well. They tend to concentrate more on the face (which liars find easier to control), followed by the body, then the voice." Men are less easily conned, because they start from a more suspicious place, and they disrespect gullibility in others.

Dates Investigated

"Did you hear about Melanie? She's having Daniel investigated by a private eye!" Not all women are gullible. According to statistics in USA Today, over 19,000 private investigators were hired in 1989, a ten percent increase over 1987. The vast majority—about 80%—of the "check-up-on-your-date clients" were single professional women in their late twenties to late forties.

Why Lie?

Research indicates women lie most often to avoid hurting other people's feelings, while men lie to enhance their self esteem. "A woman lies when she tells someone she likes something she doesn't; a man lies when he claims he's better than he is," says Michael Lewis, psychology professor at Rutgers University.

To Detect Liars

If you are fed up with being lied to, get a copy of The Lie Detector Book (Ballantine) by William J. Majeski, an ex-New York City detective. This inexpensive paperback outlines a five-step method for figuring out who's lying and who isn't. You'll learn to:

1. Study facial expressions, gestures, and body language.

2. Listen for content and sound signals such as a rise or fall in pitch.

3. Match signals with words.

4. Slow down and analyze what is being said as it's being said.

5. Ask searching questions to elicit truth.

♀♂
Aggressively Yours

Men are more aggressive toward others than women

"*Real* men are aggressive." Indeed, the cult of toughness is virtually synonymous with masculinity. The male heros of modern movies, television, and novels fight aggressively for their beliefs. Think of Rambo, John Wayne, Conan the Barbarian, Rocky. However, this aggressiveness is often fatal. According to *Omni* magazine, "more than three times as many males as females (who feel little pressure to fulfill `macho' imperatives) die from accidents, murder and suicide."

Of course, women can be aggressive, too. Some become emotionally violent when feeling resentful or rejected. Others have aggressive ways of speaking. However, this aggressiveness is much less socially acceptable. In studies on aggression, psychologist Mary Kay Biaggo found that "women are more likely to experience guilt and anxiety over aggressive impulses. For males, there is greater encouragement to express such impulses."

Studies, Studies

• **It's universal:** "The sex difference in aggression has been observed in all cultures.... Boys are more aggressive both physically and verbally. They show the attenuated forms of aggression (mock-fighting, aggressive fantasies) as well as the direct forms more frequently than girls." —Maccoby and Jacklin, Stanford researchers

• **It's nature:** "Cultural determinists insist that male aggressive behavior is the result of some sort of universal sex-role training rather than biology. Such a position is hard to defend, however, after studies such as the research by Annelise Korner, showing that even newborn male infants, who cannot yet have been exposed to sex-role training, show greater aggressiveness [than females]." —Michael Hutchison, *The Anatomy of Sex and Power*

• **It's nurture:** Studies presented at the 1991 American Anthropological Association meeting suggest that females show a strong capacity for physical aggression in cultures where it is socially acceptable. In one study, Carol Lauer studied 160 preschoolers in the U.S. and Israel. She found that while U.S. girls initiated fights much less than their male counterparts, Israeli girls used physical aggression about 20 percent more often than U.S. boys (but less than Israeli boys). "Girls and boys follow cultural dictates that can overwhelm any genetic influences," she concludes.

The Testosterone Connection

• **The male brain is tuned for aggression:** According to the authors of *Brain Sex*, "The action of the male hormones acting upon a predisposed male brain network is the root of aggression. In the opposite direction, hormones play an important part in making woman the less aggressive sex. Estrogen, for example, has a neutralizing effect on the aggression hormone, testosterone."

• **Recent findings:** Dr. John McKinlay, psychologist at the New England Research Institute, studied 1,700 men aged 40 to 70. "What we've found is that men with higher levels of testosterone correlate with a personality profile that is more forceful, aggressive, and controlling, in general, than men with lower levels of testosterone."

• **Wave of the future?:** Dr. James Dabbs of the University of Georgia is trying to determine whether testosterone has any relationship to career choice. Using a saliva test to measure testosterone levels, he's determined that actors have higher levels than ministers, and that male trial lawyers have more than other attorneys.

Time Magazine Statistics

• There are almost 17 men for every one woman doing time in prison.

• Wardens who have worked with inmates of both sexes unanimously report that women are far less aggressive and violent.

• By age 18, the average American will have seen 40,000 attempted murders and 250,000 acts of violence on TV.

⚥

Duking It Out

Women don't make war; men do

"The USA's cocky elite flying aces are patrolling the skies above the Persian Gulf, itching for a first taste of combat," writes *USA Today* on August 17, 1990. (Note the language—this *must* have been written by a man.)

Men are the war makers throughout history and across cultures (the mythic Amazons are the exception that prove the rule). The male quest for respect, power, and money, as well as a healthy dose of testosterone, leads nations to attack other countries, defend themselves against aggressors and champion lofty ideals. In *The Roots of War*, Anthony Stevens writes, "Evolution has made men expert in the arts of group violence while it has made women expert in the arts of creating and sustaining life." According to Stevens, war may be an outgrowth of cooperative hunting behavior. It may even be a biological imperative "like our capacities for sexual bonding and for providing parental care."

Women's other-focused traits foster peace, for the desire to nurture and feel intimate with others makes war untenable. True, some women support men going to war, and today, many women are in the armed services. But when polls are taken, most women oppose military adventures. "A vast and deep gender gap has been unearthed in the Persian Gulf. In one poll, 73 percent of women say they oppose war to liberate Kuwait. Only 48 percent of men concur," reported columnist Ellen Goodman during the Gulf War.

Men's Warlike Anatomy
Men are physically better equipped for war than women. According to *Wellbeing* magazine, men can run faster, jump higher, and throw farther. Men strike, hit, and kick harder. Men's grip is twice as strong as women's. Men

generally have larger bones with more cartilage in their joints, wider shoulders, and a narrower pelvis. Men eliminate metabolites such as lactic acid more efficiently, and their blood has more hemoglobin and can carry more oxygen.

Given these and other differences, it's hard to discard the idea that the difference in aggressive behavior is at least "in part physiological," writes Michael Hutchinson in *The Anatomy of Sex and Power*. Therefore, he concludes, "Serious disarmament may ultimately necessitate an increase in the proportion of women in government."

War Today, Gone Tomorrow

"As the primary victims of mechanized war, men must oppose this continued slaughter. Men need to realize that the traditional male concepts of the noble warrior are undermined and caricatured in the technological nightmare of modern warfare," writes Andrew Kimbrell in the *Utne Reader*.

Combat Comments

• "The old notion of manhood—that men are most manly when they are making a killing, whether in business or on the battlefield—is clearly destroying the whole fabric of our society." —Sam Keen, psychologist
• "Women do not suffer from the dreaded 'wimp factor.' If they support peace, their womanhood is not endangered." —Ruth Rosen, columnist
• "Never think that war no matter how necessary nor how justified is not a crime." —Ernest Hemingway, *For Whom The Bells Toll*

To Go Further

• *The Roots of War: A Jungian Perspective* (Paragon House) by Anthony Stevens is outstanding.
• Another good book is Sam Keen's *Faces of the Enemy: Reflections of the Hostile Imagination* (Harper & Row).
• See the films "Platoon," winner of the Academy Award for Best Picture in 1986, and "Born on the Fourth of July." Not all men support war, by any means.

THE
BODY SHOP

♀♂
Body Talk

Women's body language reaches out toward others more than men's

Body language is The Great Communicator. It often tells the truth better than the spoken language. When you observe people's postures, notice how women often lean toward others while men lean away. This observation is one of the best proofs that women are more other-focused than men. Leaning in is a unconscious gesture of connection, while keeping your physical distance mirrors psychological distancing. That's not the only gender body language difference though.

Gender Postures

In *Nonverbal Communication*, psychologist Shirley Weitz cites a wide range of studies on body language. Here are some of her findings:

• Men take up more space with their posture and movement; women use space in a more confining way, which is characteristic of people with less status and power.

• While conversing, women tend to move with smaller body parts—head, hands, feet. They move with more breaks at the elbow, wrist, and knuckles. They assume narrower positions. Men tend to use larger, grosser body units. They use more whole arm movements without breaks at the elbow, wrist, or knuckles. They assume wider positions.

• Women are oriented more to whom they are speaking.

• When women sit with women, they move more freely. With men, they use smaller positions. Men do not behave differently with men and women.

• Men show more periods of complete stillness.

At the Diner

For over 15 years, I've observed people's body language while eating. Here's what I've noticed:

• Women lean toward others much more than men.

- Men sit with their back against the chair more often than women; women sit with their stomach against the table more often.
- Men sit more erect and rigid; women bend over more.
- The distance between two men talking is much greater than that of two women. The distance between heterosexual couples is somewhere in between.
- As talk between women becomes more personal and emotional, the space between them decreases.

Eye Contact

Here are more findings from Shirley Weitz's book:
- Women engage in more eye contact than men. They are more sensitive to people's emotional states than men, so engage in more visual monitoring.
- Eye contact can be a signal of dominance or intimacy. Men seem to interpret initial eye contact by other males in a hostile way, while direct gazes between women often lead to greater intimacy.

Street Walkers

- When women and men approach one another on the street, women are more likely to move out of men's way and walk around them.
- When couples stand together or walk arm in arm down the street, women turn toward their lover more often than men do.
- "Men greet people with fewer lip kisses, embraces, and kinds of touch than women do," says psychologist Stephen Thayer.

Hand Jive

- Women tend to gesture more rapidly than men do, but contrary to popular belief, men speak with their hands as often as women, reports *Psychology Today*.
- Bruno Repp, an acoustics scientist at the Haskins Laboratory in Connecticut, found that men clap slower than women, but there is no difference as far as loudness.

The Decoders

- Many studies have found "women more accurate than men in 'decoding' the emotional messages that can be read from body language," says Dr. Anne Campbell in *The Opposite Sex*.

♀♂

Demystifying Men

Men's sex appeal tends to be cool; women's tends to be warm

"Who is that mystery man? What a hunk!" Men like Kevin Costner, Tom Cruise, Patrick Swayze, John F. Kennedy Jr., Robert Redford, and Sean Connery have widely applauded sex appeal. What is there about these men that drives women wild?

When you think of super sexy men, do you think of words like "charming," "challenging," "moody," "intense," "internal," "unpredictable," "sly," "tough," and "aloof," while you picture sideways glances, slow smiles, and backward-leaning postures? Men's cool sexiness is an indication of a solid (and sometimes overbearing) sense of self. They tend to hold back—both with their bodies, their facial expressions and their words. You are supposed to come to them.

On the other hand, female sex appeal tends to be warm and animated, turned out towards others. Words that come to mind are "vivacious," "eager," "external," "spunky," "soft," "attentive," and "available." Sexy women have wide-eyed expressions, ready smiles, excited speech, and forward-leaning postures. Women who epitomize this kind of appeal are Julia Roberts, Goldie Hawn, Jane Fonda, Sally Field, Teri Garr, and Debbie Reynolds. Warm sexiness is outgoing, approval-seeking and other-focused, and is the stereotypical norm for women.

Of course, there are a group of women whose appeal is more cool than warm. In the 1940s screen stars such as Greta Garbo, Hedy Lamarr, Veronica Lake, and Marlene Dietrich were groomed to mystify. Modern day women with plenty of cool are Catherine Deneuve, Faye Dunaway, and Princess Diana. And fashion models, whether they are men or women, are told to look "cool." In general, a model's look is self-focused, self-sufficient, self-possessed, and seductively sexy.

The two basic kinds of sex appeal give opposite signals about love. Extreme animation says "I am eager to love" and extreme mystery says "I am eager to be loved."

She Smiles More

In *The Opposite Sex*, Dr. Anne Campbell cites studies showing that:

• Women smile more than men, and people of both sexes smile more at women.

• Women's smiling is closely related to their need to be liked and fear that they will not be.

• Women often smile when conveying bad news and may smile so much that they defeat their goal.

• Most people think smiling indicates being in a happy mood, but "women's smiling actually seems to be linked sometimes to nervousness." (This is not to say that men don't smile when they are nervous—just that women do it more.)

• Women smile more noticeably with people they know, whereas men are more likely "to smile in fleeting public encounters—for example, with strangers on the street—women smile less when smiling could be misconstrued."

More Facial Facts

• In *Women: A Book for Men*, Wagenvoord and Bailey quote studies showing that girl babies smile more than boy babies.

• In *Non-Verbal Communication*, Shirley Weitz writes, "the basal male facial expression is closer to the neutral pole" than is a female's.

Two Things to Do

• When you are with men and women, notice which sex talks with more facial expressions.

• Ask a friend to focus on himself/herself. Then have your friend shift his/her attention to you. Which focus creates a warmer expression? Which is cooler?

♀♂

Sylvester Testosterone

Men have more testosterone
and women have more estrogen

More and more evidence suggests that sex hormones affect a wider range of behavior than previously suspected. "The more male hormone (testosterone) the fetus is exposed to, the more the adult will be male in behavior. The less amount of male hormone, the more feminine the adult behavior," explains Anne Moir in *Brain Sex*.

Other research corroborates Moir's theory. Anke A. Erhardt, professor at Columbia University, discovered that females who are exposed to higher than normal levels of testosterone before birth are more "tomboyish" as young girls. They engage in more "rough-and-tumble" behavior, like to play with boys, and are generally more competitive and aggressive.

Additionally, it is commonly known that men excel at certain spatial tasks and are better on tests of mathematical reasoning. Women, on the other hand, do better than men on certain verbal tasks and on some fine manual skills. These aptitudes seem to be influenced by the sex hormones. In a study at the University of Hamburg, researchers found that "men with higher levels of testosterone and two related hormones scored higher on tasks of spatial ability and lower on verbal fluency then men with normal levels."

Men & Hormones
• Men have about 10 times more testosterone, 1/5 the amount of estrogen, and 1/10 as much progesterone as women.
• Men have a higher sex drive than women because of testosterone.
• Testosterone is at its highest level in men just after sunrise. Men often have erections at that time.
• Testosterone levels often rise when men fight, win at sports, watch television violence, exercise, and think about sex. For

example, researchers found that men playing tennis for a $100 prize showed a rise in testosterone within a few hours after winning decisive victories.

Women & Hormones

• Women have about 5 times as much estrogen, 10 times as much progesterone, and 1/10 as much testosterone as men.

• Estrogen, which prepares the body for motherhood, is good for the arteries. It stimulates the liver to produce high density lipoproteins which help the body use up fats more efficiently and minimize the build-up of cholesterol.

• Estrogen enables women to live between 4 to 10 years longer than men because it protects against cardiovascular disease until menopause.

• Women have a better sense of smell than men, due to higher levels of estrogen.

• Many women report feeling more energetic, cheerful, and optimistic when estrogen output is at its highest—during the first half of the menstrual cycle. Conversely, they report feeling depressed and lethargic when progesterone is at its peak—the second half of the cycle.

• Estrogen assists the bones in retaining calcium. Its reduction at menopause is thought to be a major factor in the development of osteoporosis.

"High T" Women

Patricia Schreiner-Engle at New York's Mt. Sinai Medical Center studied women with higher than normal levels of testosterone. She calls them "High-T women." High-T women tend to be attracted to highly competitive, demanding careers. They are more sexually active and enjoy sex more than women with normal testosterone levels. Moreover, they have more problems in their romantic relationships with men, and are less likely to marry.

Your Own Journey

• *Women & Hormones: An Essential Guide to Being Female* (Family Publications, P.O. Box 940398; Maitland, Florida 32794) by Alice T. MacMahon, R.N., M.P.H., is a straightforward guide, full of good advice about the pill, PMS, menopause, osteoporosis, and more.

♀♂

Life in the Fat Lane

Women tend to be more concerned with weight than men

In America, approximately 24 percent of men and 27 percent of women are significantly overweight, according to the Centers for Disease Control. But even though many men have double chins and pot bellies, it's women who are dieting. In fact, according to *The Beauty Myth*, surveys show that on any given day, 25 percent of women are on diets, with 50 percent finishing, breaking or starting one.

That's because women, when they're overweight, even if it's just a few pounds, tend not to feel good about themselves. The cultural emphasis on the female body causes women, far more than men, to worry about their weight. They fall prey to the pressures of Madison Avenue and the men in their lives who equate thinness with sexual desirability, and feel inadequate if they tip the scales at anything above a model's weight.

The social pressure on women vis-a-vis weight is at the root of most eating disorders. Studies on anorexia and bulimia show that their incidence rises and falls according to society's attitude about how women should look.

Weight loss does not generally bring the love women hope for. In *Trusting Ourselves*, Dr. Karen Johnson warns, "The dieter imagines that being slender will make her a better and more desirable person. By 'improving' herself physically, she will become worthy of other people's respect and affection." However, unless women have a sense of self esteem independent of body image, they will always be at the mercy of the scale.

Fascinating Facts
• Fat makes up 15 to 18 percent of an average man's weight, and 25 to 28 percent of a woman's. And, while estimates vary, the average man's body is about 41 percent muscle,

while a woman's is 35 percent. This higher ratio of fat to muscle makes it harder for women to shed unwanted pounds.

• A survey of over 3000 students in grades five through eight by Dr. Ann C. Childress of Medical University of South Carolina revealed that 55 percent of girls and 28 percent of boys think they're fat.

• According to the *The Great Divide* by Daniel Evan Weiss, 48 percent of women surveyed versus 17 percent of men feel guilty after eating candy.

Survival of the Fattest

• "For hundreds of thousands of years of human evolution, the genes of those who are predisposed to be fat (that is, those who were predisposed to use their calories more efficiently) were selected, for these people were able to survive during food shortages. Naturally thin people simply died more often in the face of famine." —David Garner, Ph.D., researcher in eating disorders

To Explore Further

• *The Gurze Eating Disorders Bookshelf Catalog* is a wonderful resource for anyone struggling with food, body issue, self esteem, and recovery issues. Available free by calling (800) 756-7533.

• For a critique of today's most popular diet and weight loss programs, read *Diet Right!—The Consumer's Guide to Diet and Weight Loss Programs* (Conari Press) by Matthew Quincy.

• If you would like to conquer self-destructive eating patterns, read *Breaking Free From Compulsive Eating* (New American Library) by Geneen Roth. For workshops and audiotapes, contact: Breaking Free, P.O. Box 2852, Santa Cruz, CA 95063 (408) 685-8601.

• For fun, see Henry Jaglom's offbeat movie, "Eating: A Very Serious Comedy About Women & Food," in which one woman complains, "I'm still looking for a man who'll excite me as much as a baked potato."

♀♂

Right Brain, Left Brain

Men and women have
anatomical brain differences

The brains of men and women are far more similar than different, but the differences seem to be significant. Many researchers—Drs. Marie-Christine de Lacoste, Sandra Witelson, and Roger Gorski, to name a few—have reported that parts of the *corpus callosum*, the fibers that connect the right and left hemispheres of the brain, are larger in women than men, even though men's brains are larger overall. (The average male brain measures 87.4 cubic inches; the average female's, 76.8.)

Because of this difference, women use both sides of their brains together more than men do—more information is passed across women's bulkier neural pathway. "The ability to zero in on a problem with both hemispheres makes women much more perceptive about people. They are better at sensing the differences in what people say and what they mean and at picking up the nuances that reveal another person's true feelings," says Dr. Joyce Brothers.

Brain differences have also been found in the *hypothalamus*, the lusty little gland that controls the body's flow of hormones. Several researchers have confirmed that a group of neurons in the hypothalamus is more than twice as large in males as in females. This region controls the four Fs: feeding, fleeing, fighting, and . . . sex.

The interplay between structural differences and hormones causes men's thinking to be more linear—ie, goes in a straight line from A to B to C, whereas women's is more diffuse and "multidimensional." This difference makes it easier for men to focus on a task without becoming distracted (but they can get caught up in the details and forget the big picture), while women, by perceiving many different stimuli at the same time, tend to become distracted more easily, although they are able to consider the whole more comfortably.

Different Brain Structure, Different Abilities
How these differences relate to abilities is intensely debated. Nevertheless, here are two widely accepted conclusions:
Girls have greater verbal ability than boys
• Girls tend to speak earlier and articulate better than boys.
• Girls make fewer mistakes in grammar and punctuation.
• Girls tend to be better readers than boys.
Boys excel in visual-spatial and mathematical ability
• Many studies have shown males to be better at visualizing and drawing three-dimensional objects.
• Beginning at about age 12, boys' math skills increase faster than girls.

Contrary Evidence
On the SAT, overall differences have been declining. Math scores for girls in 1989 were 455—a 12 point gain during the 1980s. That gain is closing the gap between the sexes to 44 points from 53 points in 1976, reports *USA Today*. This would seem to indicate that sex role stereotypes play at least some part in boys' and girls' abilities; as gender roles have loosened, girls have felt more comfortable excelling in math.

To Go Further
• *Brain Sex: The Real Difference Between Men & Women* (A Lyle Stuart Book) by Anne Moir and David Jessel is a provocative, stimulating, and controversial book that claims most gender differences are biologically based.
• A great book that challenges the importance of biological differences between men and women is *The Mismeasure of Woman* (Simon & Schuster) by Carol Tavris. She claims that brain theories have enormous popular appeal because they fit "snugly, for example, with the Christian fundamentalist belief that men and women are innately different and thus innately designed for different roles."

♀♂
Look, Feel & Be Healthy

Women tend to be more interested in health matters than men

Women are fluent about ailments—their own and other people's. Few details are spared as they talk at length about doctor's visits, nutritional issues, and preventive cures. Interest in health is an extension of the focus women have on their physical appearance. Plus, these highly personal subject matters are grist for the talking mill as women bond over the vagaries of their bodies and minds.

In contrast, men keep health ailments to themselves. After all, it's not manly to complain about physical or mental illnesses. (However, if he's ill and wants to be nurtured, he'll complain to his mate—the one person he can trust displaying his vulnerability to.)

Because men focus less on their bodies, many eat poorly if left to their own devices. According to *In Health* magazine, men purchased 61 percent of all snack food. A 1990 Gallup poll reported that fewer than three men in ten said they felt guilty about eating unhealthy foods, while more than four in ten women expressed such feelings.

Macho Posturing

• Some men view a heart attack as a "prize," and a symbol of hard work, reports Professor Nina Rehnquist, president of the Swedish Cardiology Society. Women view a heart attack as a failure to cope with problems.

• A 1989 Lou Harris survey found that many men "thumb their noses at good-health advice." Also, when compared with women, they are less likely to wear seat belts and more likely to drive after drinking because it's a sign of toughness.

She Lives Longer

• **Life expectancy:** The average white woman can expect to live to age 78.9; black women live to 73.4. White men can expect to live to age 72.3 and black men, 64.9, reports *Monthly Vital Statistics Report.*

• **Self-inflicted damage:** "Statistics figure that one-third of the longevity gap can be attributed to the way men act. Men smoke more than women, drink more, and take more life-threatening chances. Men are murdered (usually by other men) three times as often as women are. Overall, they commit suicide at a rate of two to three times higher than that of women," writes Edward Dolnick for *In Health.*

• **The estrogen advantage:** One in five men suffer a heart attack by age 60, compared with one in 17 women, according to *The New York Times.* Women have protection against heart disease until menopause because of their higher estrogen levels. "Until puberty, boys and girls have the same cholesterol levels. But when boys hit adolescence and testosterone kicks in, their level of HDL, `good cholesterol,' plunges. In girls, HDL levels hold steady. Women maintain that advantage throughout their lives," concludes Dolnick.

• **Brain changes:** Men lose their verbal abilities two to three times faster than women as they age. Female hormones may protect the brain, according to a study by University of Pennsylvania researchers. In addition, the size of men's corpus collosum gets smaller with age, whereas the size of women's doesn't, says researcher Sandra F. Witelson.

To Go Deeper

• *The New Our Bodies, Ourselves* (Simon and Schuster) and *Ourselves, Growing Older* by Paula Brown Doress and Diana Laskin Siegal of the Boston Women's Health Book Collective are two good handbooks on women's health.

• The University of California, *Berkeley Wellness Letter* (P.O. Box 420148, Palm Coast, Florida 32142) and *The Edell Health Letter* (P.O. Box 57812, Boulder, Colorado 80322-7812; 1-800-44-EDELL) are excellent newsletters with the latest health information.

♀♂

Liquor Is Quicker

Women feel the effects of alcohol faster than men

It's true—one drink for a woman has about the same effect as two for a man. Supposedly women feel the effects of alcohol quicker because their bodies are smaller than men's and contain more fat and less water.

Researchers now have another explanation: In 1990, a team of Italian and American scientists discovered that alcohol affects women faster because women's stomach lining is far less effective than men's in breaking down alcohol. Why? Because women have much less "alcohol dehydrogenase," the stomach enzyme that breaks down alcohol before it reaches the blood stream. The enzyme theory helps explain why alcoholic women suffer more *liver damage* than alcoholic men of similar size who drink an equivalent amount. It may also explain why even small amounts of alcohol consumed during pregnancy can cause birth defects.

Why men and women drink is different, too. "While many men learn to drink as a part of the ritual of `manliness,' a greater number of women seem to drink because they feel inadequate, shy, sexually inhibited, or lacking in confidence," says Karen Johnson, Ph.D., in *Trusting Ourselves*.

She's a Codependent
Alcohol has a negative effect on more people than just the drinker. Alcoholics' families, friends, and co-workers, often suffer, too. Women tend to suffer more than men when a loved one has a drinking problem because far more men are alcoholics than women, and because they tend to endure the situation rather than leave (one out of ten husbands stay with his alcoholic wife, whereas nine out of ten wives stay with their alcoholic husband, says *Redbook*.)

In the literature on recovery, codependents—the spouses and children of alcoholics—are said to be "overly focused" on others. Consequently, advice given to codependents often sounds like this: *Don't deny your own potential in order to fill the ego needs of others. Focus more on yourself.* It's the same advice feminists give women who are self-forgetful because of socialization.

Sobering Facts

• More than 10.5 million Americans are alcoholics. About four percent of men and 14 percent of women have had a mate who is a problem drinker, reports the National Center for Health Statistics.
• According to the Bureau of the Census, in 1991, 49.3 percent of men and 23.3 percent of women in the U.S. have had five or more drinks on at least one day in the previous year.
• Between one-third and one-half of all alcoholics in the U.S. are women, according to *The Recovery Resource Book.*
• The sale of alcohol is the fourth largest source of federal revenues after corporate and individual taxes and windfall profits on oil, reports Karen Johnson, Ph.D.
• "Alcohol releases behavior our culture sees as masculine—risk-taking, aggressiveness, boisterousness. A drunken man is only too much of a good thing. A drunken woman is acting out masculine behavior; she's unnatural," writes J.S. Rudolf in *Sober Times.*

Where to Go

• For more information, call the National Council on Alcoholism and Drug Dependence, (800) 622-2255.
• *The Recovery Resource Book* (Simon and Schuster) by Barbara Yoder is a comprehensive guide that reviews more than 250 of the best books on recovery. It covers addiction to alcohol, nicotine, caffeine, sugar, food, drugs, love, sex, work, and money.
• *Codependent No More: How to Stop Controlling Others and Start Caring for Yourself* (HarperCollins) by Melody Beattie is a popular guide for codependents.

♀♂

Stress Addressed

Women have a milder response
to stress than men

We all react to stress. But here too, all is not equal. In general, "women respond better to stress," says endocrinologist Estelle Ramey.

Researchers have found that women's bodies release stress and return to normal faster than men's. For example, Swedish and American researchers studying Type A personalities found that Type A women, when problem-solving at work, respond more moderately to stress than Type A men do. The women in their study produced less adrenalin and cortisol (stress hormones), and showed less increase in heart rate and blood pressure than the men did.

Additionally, testosterone (which men have in spades) has been implicated in the stress response; it orders neuroreceptors to drop everything and react quickly. Unfortunately, it also causes men to have higher levels of low-density lipoproteins (more bad cholesterol) and increases their risk of heart disease.

Fascinating Facts

• **Crowd studies:** "Studies have found that men find it harder than women to cope when space is limited—for example, in crowds. Men in all-male crowds show more physiological signs of stress than women do in all-female crowds," says psychologist Anne Campbell.

• **Home stress:** A new study of 166 married couples by the American Psychological Association found that while men and women both bring "work stress" home, men are more likely than women to bring "home stress" to work and pick fights with co-workers as a consequence. They also found that as men withdrew from home activities due to stress, their wives took up the slack. But if wives withdrew, husbands did not compensate.

Different Emotional Reactions
• **Men retreat:** When men feel highly anxious, they tend to withdraw, becoming more closed than normal. They become less accessible and may blame others for their feelings. They are reluctant to ask for help.
• **Women open up:** When women are under stress, they reach out to others. They become more emotional and talkative. They tend to ask for help, not only from friends and family, but also from therapists and clergy. They don't always react positively, however, because they tend to blame themselves for whatever is going on. They may also become depressed.

The Depression Factor
"Studies have consistently found that women's risk of depression exceeds that of men by a ratio of two to one," according to the American Psychological Association's National Task Force on Women and Depression. In addition, "approximately 70 percent of all prescriptions for antidepressants are given to women, but often with improper diagnosis and monitoring. Depression in women is misdiagnosed at least 30-50 percent of the time."

Why do more women get depressed? There are many complex reasons but socialization and biology seem to play a part. "Men, the hunters, were more likely to have benefitted from elaborate and fast-acting stress mechanisms in the presence of danger. And women, the nurturers, were more likely to have benefitted from an *emotional* responsiveness to their environment. Depression (female response) and the effects of continuous stress (male response) may be the prices they pay for these legacies: an integral part of our maleness and femaleness," say the authors of *Sex and the Brain*.

To Go Further
• If you are caught in the frantic pace of today's world, read *Stressed Out? A Guidebook for Taking Care of Yourself* (Health Communications) by Brian Robinson, Ph.D.

♀♂
Pretty Woman

Women are more concerned about their looks than men

"How do I look?" Women's self-worth is firmly tied to their physical appearance. Magazine and television advertising exerts tremendous pressure on women to look good (and sexy). From early childhood, women learn to focus on their looks and are generally disappointed with what they find. How many women do you know who are content with their appearance?

As a rule, men care less about their looks. Men seldom talk about clothes, hair styles, mousse, or after-shave lotions. Men's self-esteem is linked more to performance than appearance. Consequently, many men think primping is for wimps. For example, only about 15 percent of Vidal Sassoon's hair coloring business in L.A. is men and these men fear exposure, asking for private rooms and after-hours appointments.

It is somewhat socially acceptable, however, for men to be concerned with going bald. However, most of that concern takes place in private. Despite the use of remedies to deal with the problem (more than two million men have used Rogaine, a hair restorer, since 1988), you rarely hear men complaining together about going bald or suggesting remedies to one another.

Writer Gloria Steinem says, "Many surveys show that women generally think they look worse than they do—but men think they look better than they do. So we both need to become more realistic." Her observation is confirmed by a survey in *The Great Divide* by Daniel Evan Weiss—42 percent of men as opposed to only 28 percent of women consider themselves handsome or pretty.

Physique Critique
In 1991, *Longevity* magazine did a survey of the sexual

secrets of over 2000 baby boomers. Here are some of the results vis-a-vis bodies:

• What men dislike most in women: large hips (59%); facial wrinkles (51%); gray hair (41%); short legs (33%); small breasts (25%).

• What women dislike most in men: portly body (70%); baldness (49%); shortness (48%); love handles (47%); facial wrinkles (12%).

Mostly Women

• The average woman uses 17 to 21 grooming and beauty products in her morning routine, reports dermatologist Paul Lazar, M.D., of Northwestern University.

• The average woman brushes, combs, or checks her hair about five times a day, which takes about 36 minutes, according to studies by the Upjohn Hair Information Center.

• In a *Self* survey, 68% of women respondents agreed, "The way you look strongly affects the way you feel and act."

• About two million American women have breast implants, 80 percent for cosmetic reasons, reports *USA Today*. Recently the safety of such implants has been seriously questioned.

Mostly Men

• The Georgette Klinger facial salon in Manhattan claims that about 20 percent of its clientele are men.

• One in four nose jobs is performed on men, says *Men's Health*.

• More than three million men color their own hair, spending over $47 million dollars a year, says Julie Bohl, a spokesperson for Grecian Formula 16.

• Sixty-eight percent of men like the way they look naked, compared with only 22 percent of women, reports *In Health*.

Your Own Journey

• To find out how the diet, cosmetics, and fashion industries manipulate women, read Naomi Wolf's controversial book, *The Beauty Myth* (William Morrow and Company). Wolf says, "We are in the midst of a violent backlash against feminism that uses images of female beauty as a political weapon against women's advancement."

WHAT'S HOT, WHAT'S NOT

♀♂
The Career Scene

More than women,
men define themselves by their jobs

Work is emotionally important to both men and women. But because women value and have strong friendships and family life, they tend to be less closely identified with their work than men are. On the other hand, men, being action-oriented, prove themselves at work and are more affected by what happens at the office than women. If a man wins at work, he feels elated; when he loses, he feels depressed.

"Most often, men feel devastated and worthless when they have been severely affected by a lack of career success or when they have had a major financial setback. Women can find satisfaction in their lives if they have rewarding relationships with people," says psychologist Morton H. Shaevitz.

Business and politics were created in men's image. Men's whole life, from childhood on, is about playing power games. Men's mannerisms—ways of speaking, gesturing, standing, and sitting—are more aggressive than women's. And the work world reflects those values. "The world of work is essentially a world of competition which forces the ego into consciousness, " notes Esther M. Harding in *The Way of All Women*.

To succeed in a man's world, women have had to act like men. Yet, if they do, they are accused of being unfeminine and pushy. In *Working With Men*, Beth Milwid, Ph.D., says, "Although some women reported allowing themselves the freedom to bring feminine characteristics into their lives at work, others still feel uncomfortable appearing `too soft' on the job." Notes writer Susan Waggoner, "Career women face the difficult problem of making it in a man's world without ruffling too many male egos on the way up."

There is some indication this female conundrum is

changing. More and more women are creating situations in which they can be themselves, and the feminine style of leadership at work is gaining more attention and praise.

Performance Pressure

• "When men try to kill themselves, it is commonly out of an injured sense of pride or competence, often related to work. When women attempt suicide, it is usually because of failures involving lovers, family, or friends." —Anastasia Toufexis, writer

Juggling Two Careers

• Writer Gloria Steinem says men and women won't truly be equal "unless men, too, are saying `How can I juggle two careers?'"

• "Women, newly liberated, have discovered how difficult it is to balance their career with their personal life. I don't know why they're so surprised. Men have historically been failures at this."—a character in Henry Jaglom's film, "Someone to Love"

The Grim Facts

• **She's typical:** On average, women earn 71 cents to every dollar a man earns, reports the Census Bureau. The pay gap reflects lower salaries paid in fields traditionally dominated by women and the difficulty women have breaking through the "glass ceiling" to higher paid positions.

• **The executives:** The ten highest paid male executives in the U.S. make two to ten times what top-paid female executives earn. Best paid women work in the fashion, cosmetics, and retail industries, according to *USA Today*.

To Go Further

• *Working With Men—Professional Women Talk About Power, Sexuality, and Ethics* (Beyond Words Publishing, Inc.) by Beth Milwid, Ph.D. "One of the best studies of women in business yet published," says the *San Francisco Chronicle*.

• *The Female Advantage* (Doubleday) by Sally Helgesen argues that women's management style is different—and better in many cases—than men's.

♀♂
Riding the Edge

Men take more physical risks than women

It's generally men who want to go higher, deeper, and faster. The first person to climb Mt. Everest was a man. Ditto the first airplane pilot, moon walker, parachute jumper, bullfighter, trapeze artist etc., etc. Over the years, men have come up with an incredible menu of wild and crazy adventures that at least some of them engage in—spelunking, bungee jumping, hang-gliding, boxing, auto and speedboat racing, to name a few. Men enjoy physical risks because they're competitive (records can be broken), they're a way to get respect and attention, and they offer a chance to bond with other men doing the same thing.

Dangerous pursuits are aggressive acts, perhaps prompted by testosterone. Some psychologists, claims Dr. Anne Campbell in *The Opposite Sex*, say that both aggression and rough physical play result from the general vigor and activity testosterone provides. "Boys expend energy at a higher rate than girls," she notes, "particularly in social situations."

Of course, not all men love physical risks, and certainly some women do have the urge to risk, too. Think of Amelia Earhart, Sally Ride, and Sharon Adams (the first woman to sail alone across the Pacific Ocean). But these women are clearly in the minority.

Daring Data
In *The Great Divide: How Females & Males Really Differ*, author Daniel Weiss cites a survey that shows:

• Twenty-eight percent of the men and 16 percent of the women would like to climb Mt. Everest.

• Eleven percent of males and 5 percent of females would like to make an "Evil Knievel" jump on a motorcycle.

• Thirty-seven percent of males and 20 percent of females would like to parachute out of a plane.

• Forty-seven percent of men and 21 percent of women would like to race a car in the Indianapolis 500.

• Fifty-seven percent of males and 41 percent of females would like to be transported 100 years into the future.

T is for Risk-Taking

What do Evil Knievel and Albert Einstein have in common? Both are risk-takers, says University of Wisconsin psychologist Frank Farley. In 25 years of studying risk-taking, he has come to regard seeking new knowledge and seeking new frontiers (i.e., taking physical risks) as part of the same personality trait. He has defined a continuum of behavior ranging from those who avoid risk (Type t) to those who seek it (Type T). How we relate to our work and our personal lives can be measured by where we fall on the scale. "If you're a Type t working on daily deadlines . . . you'd probably be overwhelmed, unhappy and ineffective. However, a Type T would thrive there because it's not necessarily stress to them. It's excitement."

Comfort Zone

• "What we have is based on moment-to-moment choices of what we *do*. In each of these moments we choose. We either take a risk and move toward what we want, or we play it safe and choose comfort. Most of the people, most of the time, choose comfort." —John-Roger and Peter McWilliams, *Life 101*.

To Go Further

• Watch ESPN for men (and women) doing exciting and dangerous things. You'll see events such as the rodeo competitions in which men named Cody Custer, Clint Branger and Tuff Hedeman ride bucking bulls.

• Read *Why the Reckless Survive . . . and Other Secrets of Human Nature* (Penguin) by Melvin Konner.

• Check out the new book, *Women & Risk: How to Master Your Fears and Do What You Never Thought You Could Do* (St. Martin's) by Nicky Marone.

• Another good resource is Ralph Keyes' book, *Chancing It: Why We Take Risks* (Little, Brown).

♀♂

The Joy of Shopping

In general, women enjoy shopping much more than men do

"Let's go shopping, Jennifer!" Many women's idea of fun is shopping with a friend, going to lunch, then shopping some more. Whew! It makes most men tired just to think about a day at the mall. "Women frequently hang out in malls for recreation; men want to accomplish their goal—and get out," writes Jeanne Stein in the *Los Angeles Times*.

To many women, shopping—especially for clothes and items for the home—is a joyful experience. "Most women perceive shopping as an experience of discovery. Most men approach it as a task, not an adventure," says Joe Tanenbaum in *Male & Female Realities*. While men usually look for known products and styles, women often seek items that are new and different. That's why women's fashions change seasonally. Women are "enlivened and re-energized by new sights, sounds, and aromas" in shopping environments, notes Tanenbaum.

Some men hate shopping so much that they let their wives or girlfriends buy all their clothes. One man told me, "If my wife brings home clothes I don't like, I have her take them back and buy something I might like better." Now that's service! Another told me, "When my pants get tight, I eat less, so I don't have to go shopping for a bigger size."

Shopping trips with women make certain men highly anxious. We're talking BPA—Borderline Panic Attack. After being in a department store for less than five minutes, they feel the walls are closing in on them. Savvy store owners place a comfortable sofa and a basket of magazines inside their store for boyfriends/husbands.

Women, more than men, are bargain hunters. They love to find a good deal and then boast about it. Men like to point out: "You'd save more by staying home!"

Fascinating Facts
• "Seventy-two percent of females and 44 percent of males consider shopping pleasurable." —Daniel Evan Weiss, *The Great Divide—How Females & Males Really Differ*
• In the U.S. 130 million people visit a shopping mall at least once a week—and 70 percent of them are women, reports the International Council of Shopping Centers.
• "They came, they saw, they shopped."—Berlin Wall graffiti

When He Shops
• "The men's department in a department store is always on the first floor, two inches from the door, so hopefully they'll see it from the parking lot. I think a drive-through store for men would be really good." —Rita Rudner, comedian
• The percentage of male shoppers is increasing, says Robert Sommers, director of the Center for Consumer Research at the University of California at Davis. "Some men are quite turned on by shopping. They're using their mathematical skills in comparing prices and brands and turning it into a different sort of experience that is less subjective and impulse-oriented."

Are You a Shopaholic?
• Do you find yourself watching the Home Shopping channel for excitement? Are your credit cards always at their limits? Do you get antsy when environmentalists talk about how consumerism is destroying the planet? If so, you may be a compulsive shopper. To overcome the urge to splurge, read Carol Wesson's *Women Who Shop Too Much* (St. Martin's Press). Wesson says you're headed for trouble, if you "spend more and more time shopping without a clear cut purpose or need," if you "think about shopping obsessively," and if you feel "guilty and ashamed after spending or shopping."

♀♂
Feminism Revisited

Women's roles have changed more than men's in the past three decades

Both men and women have made role changes over the years, but women's changes have far outstripped men's. "In a mere 25 years, American women have changed the whole nature of society," says Michael Korda in *Male Chauvinism*. Women work more outside the home than they used to and women have entered into many careers that were traditionally considered "male"; according to the Census Bureau, women currently make up 20.6% of architects, 22.2% lawyers and 38.7% of college and university teachers. And the number of women-owned businesses in the U.S. increased from 26,120 in 1982 to 41,148 in 1987.

Additionally, more women have defined their lives apart from men. For example, many women are choosing to have children on their own. In 1987, there were 2.6 million never-married women raising children under 21 whose fathers were not living with them, according to the Department of Health and Human Services.

Men have also begun to see their role differently, particularly vis-a-vis childrearing. There are about 257,000 stay-at-home dads—which make up about two percent of married parents with children under 18, reports the U.S. Labor Department.

Facing the Facts

"American women have a long way to go before they reach the promised land of equality," says Susan Faludi in *Backlash: The Undeclared War Against Women*. Here are some facts she cites:

• Eighty percent of working women are still stuck in traditional "female" jobs.

• In the Reagan years, sex discrimination charges rose nearly 25 percent while complaints of sexual harassment jumped almost

70 percent.

- The number of rapes have more than doubled since the early 70s and nearly half of all homeless women are refugees of domestic violence.

Women and Political Power

- Women make up about 53 percent of voters, but in 1991, there were only two female senators and three female governors.
- Columnist William Safire says many women "are letting down their [gender] by not demanding more female candidates and by not supporting them when they run."
- An Iowa group, The Fund for the Feminist Majority, is calling for "gender balance" laws, which would make it mandatory for the governor to appoint equal numbers of men and women to all state boards and commissions.

Financial Realities

- According to 1989 U.S. Census data, 57.4 percent of displaced homemakers and 47.6 percent of single mothers experience poverty or near poverty.
- In the year following divorce, a woman's standard of living falls about 73 percent, while the man's rises 42 percent, reported The Almanac of the American People in 1988.

The Men's Movement

All across the nation, thousands of (mostly white) men are getting together to share feelings and talk about personal issues such as: "Where was my dad when I was growing up?"; "Why do I feel unsatisfied with my work?; "What does it mean to be a man in modern society?" The unofficial leaders of the men's movement are poet Robert Bly, who wrote *Iron John* (Addison-Wesley) and Sam Keen, author of *Fire In The Belly: On Being A Man* (Bantam Books). Both writers urge men to use their masculine strength for good, not greed.

To Go Deeper

- For a compassionate discussion of men's issues, subscribe to the free quarterly, *Wingspan: Journal of the Male Spirit* (Box 1492, Manchester, MA 01944).
- To learn about women's concerns, subscribe to the new *Ms.*, PO Box 57122, Boulder, CO 80321. Without advertising, it's better than ever.

♀♂

Take This Job, Please

Women still do far more housework and child care than men

Women still shoulder 70 percent of the household duties, even if they work full time. In the 1980s, many women were called "Superwomen" because they juggled a career, children, a husband, and homemaking duties. Women were fascinated with the possibility of being, doing, and having more than women in the past. In the 1990s, many women are more realistic about what they can accomplish—and they're more eager than ever for men to help.

The Second Shift

In a landmark study, sociologist Arlie Hochschild went into the homes of today's two-career families to observe what goes on at the end of the "work day." Overwhelmingly, she discovered that it's the woman who's doing the lion's share of the work. Here are some of her findings, taken from her fascinating book, *The Second Shift:*

• Only 20 percent of men shared housework equally.

• Men did fewer of the "undesirable" chores such as cleaning the bathroom.

• Although most women accepted the inequity to "keep the peace," they tend to suffer chronic exhaustion, low sex drive, and more frequent illnesses.

• Few employers offer flex-time, parental leave, or child care. We need "a society humanely adapted to the fact that most women work outside the home," urges Hochschild.

The result of this great inequity, says Hochschild, is that both partners suffer. "I came to realize that those husbands who helped very little at home were often indirectly just as deeply affected as their wives by the need to do that work, through the resentment their wives feel

144

toward them, and through their need to steel themselves against that resentment."

Notable Quotes

• "One of the hard won prizes of the Women's Movement is the right to become terminally exhausted."—Erica Jong
• "At best, marriage is not an institution that favors women. Whether we stay at home or whether we have jobs, it remains a given even today that the kids, the house, and making one's husband comfortable are basically our responsibilities."—Meredith Baxter Birney

Giving Up Control

How much of women's overwork stems from women's inclination to nurture and how much comes from living with outdated models of what a wife and mother should be? So what if the beds are unmade, if the kids grab their own cereal in the morning, the trash sits there a day longer? I've heard many women complain about all the housework they have to do and then refuse to "let" their children and husbands participate because "they don't do it right" (i.e., the way the woman would).

Ellen Galinsky of the Families and Work Institute claims there are three things that predict whether men and women will share housework equally: if the woman believes strongly such work should be divided, if she is willing to accept that her husband might do things differently, and if she earns as much or more than he.

Changing Things

• **Women:** If you're working circles around him at home, do less and ask him to do more.
• **Men:** It's time to do your fair share. She'll be less resentful if you chip in with more than just the chores you'd rather do.
• **Both:** Read *Simply Organized!* (Berkley) by Connie Cox and Cris Evatt. This inexpensive paperback is full of household hints that will help you live more simply in spite of your myriad responsibilities.

♀♂
Reel Life

Movies cater more to male than female audiences

"Let's go to a movie! How about 'Harley Davidson and the Marlboro Man'?" If you're a man, you have more movies to choose from than women do. The movie industry claims it's catering to its audience—males aged 16 to 25 make up the largest movie-going audience, according to *USA Today*—but perhaps that's because the subject matter of most films attracts these men and boys. (Why can't we have more coming-of-age films like "Stand By Me," "ET" or even "Home Alone" that feature a girl?)

It certainly is true that women are more willing to see films such as "Rambo" than men are willing to sit through "Fried Green Tomatoes." The other-focusedness of women makes them more interested in the experiences of the opposite sex, while men tend to need more similarity to identify with.

Meryl, Cher & Callie

• "Instead of targeting macho males, the studios should ask, 'Who's deliberately staying home?'" —Meryl Streep
• "I wish there were more films like 'Dances with Wolves,' 'Terms of Endearment,' and 'Moonstruck' to balance 'Total Recall,' 'Lethal Weapon,' and 'Die Hard.' If today's movies reflect society, someone should call the paramedics." — Cher
• "Films never deal with the incredible amount of anger women feel about the victimization of their gender." — Callie Khouri, screenwriter for "Thelma and Louise" (that sought to remedy the problem)

She Picks Jerks

"It is becoming routine for female leads to begin films with all manner of jerk boyfriends," says Michael MacCambridge, writing for the Cox News Service. "The implication of these smart women repeatedly making foolish choices is that modern women are still co-dependent and passive, wallowing around in any relationship until they're miraculously saved by the right man at the right time." Films with this theme include "Postcards from the Edge,""Sleeping with the Enemy," and "Crossing Delancey." Blame (mostly male) screenwriters for these films.

Older Women in Movies
Older women are portrayed quite differently from men and younger women. Researchers Carol Taylor and Elizabeth Markson found that:

• Men in the movies who get older are seen as distinguished, while women are seen as old.

• When given significant roles, older women are cast as nurturers to men or families.

• Men who earned the best actor award averaged 45 years of age while their female counterparts averaged 35.

Tough Woman Trend?
In 1991, three major films featured gun-toting female leads: "Thelma and Louise," "Terminator II," and "V.I. Warshawski." What this means for future films remains to be seen.

Men's Role Models
Men may rule the screen, but their roles don't tend to be any healthier than women's. "Macho movies of the `Rambo' and `Robocop' extreme appeal to boys who are desperately seeking their elusive masculinity. If these are gender training films for the next decade, I'm worried," says Frank Pittman, M.D., in the *Networker*.

Writer Joe Baltake concurs, "Movies are providing some pretty lousy role models of what being a man means." Maybe, the men's movement will encourage filmmakers to show men's softer, more nurturing side. Are "The Doctor," "The Fisher King," and "Regarding Henry" harbingers of things to come?

WRAPPING
IT UP

♀♂
The Differences

Here's a summary of the male and female personality traits you've read in this book. By getting to know these traits, you'll hopefully understand yourself and others better. You'll be able to distinguish between a person's "gender" traits and their "individual" traits--a useful skill for both personal and business relationships. Read the traits horizontally to compare men and women; then read vertically to get a sense of maleness and femaleness.

He:	She:
More self-focused	More other-focused
Needs less intimacy	Needs more intimacy
Fears engulfment	Fears abandonment
Feels less resentful	Feels more resentful
Needs less approval	Needs more approval
Stronger identity	Weaker identity
More independent	Less independent
Often detached	Often emotional
An attention-getter	An attention-giver
Highly competitive	Less competitive
Strong drive for power/money	Power/Money less important
Respect very important	Respect less important
Often obsessed with sports	Sports less important
Talks mostly about "things"	Talks mostly about "people"
Less talkative in private	Less talkative in public
Takes things literally	Looks for hidden meanings
Language more direct	Language more indirect
Less responsive listener	More responsive listener
Decisions made quicker	Takes more time to decide
Gossips less	Gossips more
Engages in put-downs	Engages in backbiting
Focuses more on solutions	Likes to discuss problems

Less apologetic	More apologetic
Tells more jokes/stories	Tells fewer jokes/stories
Less willing to seek help	Seeks help readily
Boasts about performance	Boasts less frequently
Nags less often	Nags more often
Often intimidates others	Seldom intimidates others
Issues orders	Makes suggestions
Often seeks conflict	Tends to avoid conflict
Likes to be adored	Likes to adore others
Fearful of commitment	Eager for commitment
Sexually jealous of mate	Emotionally jealous of mate
Accepts others more	Tries to change others more
Thrives on receiving	Thrives on giving
More polygamous	More monogamous
More sadistic	More masochistic
More sex-oriented	More love-oriented
Has fewer close friends	Has many close friends
Likes group activities	Prefers intimate encounters
Worries less about others	Worries more about others
More sensitive to stress	Less sensitive to stress
Less trusting	Often too trusting
More aggressive	Less aggressive
Initiates war	Does not make war
Posture leans back more	Posture leans forward more
Cooler/seductive sexiness	Warmer/animated sexiness
Has more testosterone	Has more estrogen
Less into dieting	More into dieting
Less concerned about health	More concerned about health
Worries less about appearance	Worries more about appearance
Takes more physical risks	Takes fewer physical risks
Shops out of necessity	Often shops for enjoyment

♀♂
The Gender Tenscale

In the first chapter, I noted that individual male and female traits are best seen on a continuum. Here's a one-to-ten scale to help you understand men and women better.

Tens—the Extremes (The Batterer, The Battered)

These extremely self-focused men and other-focused women hurt themselves and/or others in a variety of ways. This category includes people with complicated psychological problems. The men cannot control their rage, tend to be paranoid, and may be highly reclusive. The women are highly dependent and emotional.

Sevens, Eights, Nines—the Heavies (The Jerk, Macho Man, The Doormat, Miss Too-Nice, Mrs. Mother Everyone)

These heavily self-focused men and other-focused women are like the folks above, but to a lesser degree. Their behavior is a caricature of their gender—the traits in this book fit them virtually perfectly, one for one. These men give women a hard time and these women allow themselves to be pushed around. These women tend to love men too much and these men tend to seek adoration and avoid commitment.

Threes, Fours, Fives, Sixes—the Moderates (The Average Person)

These men are moderately self-focused, so are able to focus on others, too—about 25 to 35 percent of the time. The women are moderately other-focused, so do have sense of self that is evident, but not highly developed. The moderates do not display every single one of the traits common to their gender; in some ways, they take after the opposite sex.

Ones, Twos—the Lights (Mr. Supercaring, The Nice Guy, The Self-Reliant Woman)

These lightly self-focused men and lightly other-focused women are almost balanced—their overall focus on self and others is nearly equal. These men are warmer and more nurturing than the average man, and these women are cooler and less emotional than the average woman. Both tend to think clearly and creatively about most issues because they have a choice about giving to self versus giving to others.

Opposites Attract

It's a natural fact: opposites tend to attract. Men and women tend to be sexually attracted to the people who are in the same general position on the tenscale as they are. This goes for both lovers and friends. For example, Joe Macho will probably fall for Ms. Doormat, and his friends will be Rambo-types like himself. Likewise, Mr. Supercaring will be attracted to Ms. Self-Reliant, and their friends will be like them, too.

♀♂
What's Your Score?

Here are the answers to the test you took on page 10.

1. False	16. True
2. False	17. False
3. True	18. False
4. False	19. True
5. False	20. True
6. False	21. True
7. True	22. False
8. True	23. False
9. False	24. False
10. True	25. True
11. False	26. False
12. True	27. True
13. True	28. False
14. True	29. True
15. False	30. False

Excellent . . . . 28-30 correct

Good . . . . 25-27 correct

Fair . . . . 21-24 correct

Thank You, Folks!

Adams, Virginia. "Getting at the Heart of Jealous Love." *Psychology Today.* May 1980, pg. 38.

Alexander, Shana. *When She Was Bad.* New York: Dell, 1991.

Allis, Sam. "What Do Men Really Want?" Time, Fall 1990. pg. 80.

Baer, Jean. *How to Be an Assertive (Not Aggressive) Woman.* New York: A Signet Book, 1976.

Baldwin, Dr. Bruce A. "The Competition Compulsion." *U.S. Air,* April 1990, pp. 28-35.

Barash, David, zoologist. *The Whispering Within.* New York: Harper & Row, 1979.

Barbieri, Susan M. "An Affair to Forget." *Orlando Sentinel.* 1991.

Barker, Robert L. *The Green Eyed Marriage.* New York: Free Press, 1987.

Barry, Dave. *Dave Barry's Greatest Hits.* New York: Fawcett, 1988.

Bass, Allison. "Eating Disorders: Societies Revenge on Women." *Boston Globe.* December 28, 1991.

Beck, Aaron T., M.D. *Love is Never Enough.* New York: Harper and Row, 1988.

Bellinger, David C., and Jean Berko Gleason. "Sex Differences in Directives to Young Children." *Sex Roles: A Journal of Research,* Vol. 8, No. 11, November 1982, p. 1123.

Benbow, Camilla Persson. "Sex Differences in Mathematical Ability: Fact or Artifact?" *Science,* December 1980.

Berkowitz, Bob with Gittines, Roger. *What Men Won't Tell You But Women Need To Know.* New York: William Morrow, 1990.

Blakeslee, Sandra., "The True Story Behind Breast Implants." *Glamour.* August 1991.

Bloom, Lynn Z., Karen Coburn, Joan Perlman. *The New Assertive Woman.* New York: Dell, 1975. p.121

Bly, Robert. *Iron John.* Reading, Massachusetts: Addison-Wesley, 1990.

Bohl, Julie, Quoted in "Losing It" by Gaile Robinson. *Los Angeles Times,* 1991.

Bower, Bruce. "Darwin's Minds." *Science News,* Vol. 140. Oct. 12, 1991. pg. 232-234.

Braiker, Harriet B. *Getting Up When You're Feeling Down.* New York: Putnam, 1988.

Brody, Robert. "Psych Outs." *Men's Health,* Spring 1989, p. 62.

Brothers, Dr. Joyce. *What Every Women Should Know About Men.* New York: Simon and Schuster, 1981 pp. 17, 40, 261.

Browder, Sue. "Man vs. Woman." *Woman*. Sept. 1990 p. 22.

Brown, Richard, film professor. Quoted in "Few movies have the feminine touch" by Dottie Enrico. *The Contra Costa Times*, Oct. 16, 1990.

Butler, Pamela E. *Self-Assertion for Women.* San Francisco: Harper & Row, 1981.

Campbell, Anne. *The Opposite Sex*. Topsfield, MA: Salem House, 1989.

Cannon, Dyan, "Dyan Cannon" by Richard Meryman. *Lear's*. January 1991 p. 71.

Carter, Stephen & Julia Sokol. *Men Who Can't Love*. New York: Berkeley Publishing, 1988.

Cher, actress. "Cher Today" by Jim Jerome. *People*. January 21, 1991. p. 78.

Chodorow, Nancy. *Women, Culture and Society*. Stanford: Stanford University Press, 1974.

Collins, Joan. *Past Imperfect*. New York: Berkeley Books, 1985.

Crisp, Quentin. "Idle Chatter." *Lear's*. June 1990, p.72.

Darling, Lyn. "Finally, We Can Deal With Authority Figures." *Self*, September 1990, p.217.

Davis, Flora. "How to Read Men," *Woman's Day*, November 15, 1983.

Davis, Susan. "Ruled by Hormones." *San Francisco Examiner*, November 7, 1990.

DeAngelis, Barbara, Ph.D. *Secrets About Men Every Woman Should Know. New York: Delacorte Press*, 1990.

Druck, Dr, Ken. *The Secrets Men Keep*. New York: Ballantine Books, 1985.

Dunaway, Diane & Jonathan Kramer. *Why Men Don't Get Enough Sex and Women Don't Get Enough Love*. New York: Pocket Books, 1990.

Edwards, Owen. "On Being A New Man," *Cosmopolitan*, p. 170.

Eichenbaum, Louise and Orbach, Susie. *Between Women*. New York: Penquin Books, 1987.

Ellsworth, P. and Ross, L. "Intimacy in response to direct gaze." *Journal of Experimental Social Psychology*, 1975.

Evatt, Cris and Feld, Bruce. *The Givers and the Takers*. New York: Fawcett, 1988.

Evert, Chris. "My Love Match With Andy." *Good Housekeeping*, October 1990, p. 86.

Faludi, Susan. *Backlash: The Undeclared War Against American Women*. New York: Crown Publishers, 1991.

Farrell, Warren, Ph.D. *Why Men Are The Way They Are*. New York: Berkeley books, 1986.

Fasteau, Marc Feigen. *The Male Machine*. New York: McGraw-Hill Book Company, 1974.

Fisher, Roger and William Ury. *Getting to Yes*. New York: Penquin Books, 1983.

Forbes, Dinah. "Women and Men: Is It Possible to Get Along?"

Utne Reader, Nov./Dec. 1990, p. 85, 86.

Fraser, Antonia. *Love Letters*. Contemporary Books, Inc. 1989.

Friedman, Roberta. "Hand Jive." *Psychology Today*. June 1988.

Friedman, Sonja. *Men are Just Desserts*. New York: Warner Books, 1983.

Friedan, Betty. *The Second Stage*. New York: Summit Books, 1981.

Garai, J.E. and Scheinfeld, A. *Genetic Psychology Monographs*, 1968, pp. 77, 169-229.

Garfinkel, Perry. *In A Man's World*. New York: New American Library, 1985.

Garner, David, Ph.D. "Rent a New Thinner Body." *Radiance*. Winter 1991, p. 37.

Gilligan, Carol. *In A Difference Voice*. Cambridge, MA: Harvard University Press, 1982.

Gish, Annabeth. "The Dish on Gish" by Nikki Finke. *Mademoiselle*, April 1990, p.100.

Glantz, Kalman and Pearce, John K. *Exiles From Eden*. New York: W.W. Norton & Company, 1989.

Goldberg, Herb, Ph.D. *The New Male Female Relationship*. New York: New American Library, 1983.

____*What Men Really Want*. New York: A Signet Book, 1991.

Goenka, S.N. *Vipassana Meditation*. San Francisco: Harper & Row, 1987.

Gonick, Jean. "Girl Talk." *Glamour*. August 1990, p. 227.

Gray, John. *Men, Women And Relationships*. Hillsborough, Oregon: Beyond Words Publishing, Inc. 1990.

Gumbel, Bryant. "Today's Man." *McCall's*, June 1987, p. 69.

Hall, J. "Gender effects in decoding nonverbal cues." *Psychological bulletin*, 1978.

Halpern, Howard M. Ph.D. *How To Break Your Addiction To A Person*. New York: Bantam Books, 1982.

Hamill, Pete. "What Men Talk About When They Talk About Women." *Cosmopolitan*. April 1988, p. 219

Hamlin, Sonja. *How To Talk So People Will Listen*. New York: Harper & Row, 1988.

Harding, M. Esther. *The Way of All Women*. New York: Harper & Row Publishers, Inc., 1970.

Harrison, Barbara Grizzuti. "Is sisterhood still powerful?" *Cosmopolitan*, April 1990, p. 154.

Haskell, Molly. *From Reverence To Rape*. Chicago: University of Chicago Press.

Hayes, Jody. *Smart Love*. Los Angeles: Jeremy P. Tarcher, 1989.

Hemingway, Ernest. *For Whom The Bells Toll*. New York: Charles Scribner's & Sons, 1940. p. 236.

Hite, Shere. *The Hite Report: Women and Love*. New York: Alfred K. Knopf, 1987.

Hochschild, Arlie. *The Second Shift*. New York: Avon Books, 1989.

Hood, Ann. "The Answer Couple." *Glamour.* July 1990, p. 97.

Hutchison, Michael. *The Anatomy of Sex and Power.* New York: William Morrow and Company, 1990.

Irby, Christopher. "Girl Talk, Boy Talk." *Cosmopolitan.* May 1988.

Jaffe, Dennis, Ph.D. *Working with the Ones You Love.* Emeryville, CA: Conari Press, 1991.

James, Jennifer, Ph.D. *Success is the Quality of Your Journey.* New York: Newmarket Press, 1983.

Jemmott, John III, Ph.D. "They're Life Shortening." *Longevity.* October 1990, p.18.

Johnson, Kaufman Lee. "Let's Talk." *Contra Costa Times,* October 16, 1990.

Johnson, Karen and Ferguson, Tom. *Trusting Ourselves: The Sourcebook on Psychology for Women.* New York: Atlantic Monthly Press, 1990.

Jong, Erica. *Any Women's Blues.* New York: Harper and Row, 1990.

Kaplan, Janice. "The Trouble with Co-Dependency." *Self.* July 1990.

Karen, Bob. "How and When do Men Decide To Marry?" *Cosmopolitan,* July 1990. p. 180.

Kassorla, Irene C., Ph.D. *Go For It.* New York: Dell, 1984.

Keen, Sam. *Fire In The Belly.* New York: Bantam, 1991.

Khouri, Callie. Quoted in *Glamour.* August 1991, p. 142.

Kitzinger, Shiela. *Women's Experience of Sex.* New York: Penguin, 1985.

Konner, Melvin. *Why the Reckless Survive...and Other Secrets of Nature.* New York: Penguin Books, 1990.

Korda, Michael. *Male Chauvinism.* New York: Random House, 1972.
_____. The Feminist Revolution." *Cosmopolitan,* May 1990, p. 327.

Krupnick, Catherine, Ed.D. "Women Outalked in Class," *Glamour,* August 1990. p. 92.

Lakoff, Robin Tolmach. *Talking Power.* Basic Books, 1990.

Lever, Janet. "Sex Differences in the Games Children Play." *Social Problems* 23 (1976): 478-483.

Levinson, R., & Gottman J. (1985) *Journal of Personality and Social Psychology.* pp. 49, 85-94.

Levitt, Shelley. "Why Women Cheat." *New Woman,* October 1990.

Levy, Jerre. *Cerebral Correlations of Conscious Experience.* New York: North Holland Publishing, Co., 1978.

Lindbergh, Anne Morrow, *Gift From The Sea.* New York: Vinatage Edition, 1978.

Linquist, Dr. Luann. *Secret Lovers.* Lexington, MA: Lexington Books, 1989.

Lykken, David T. "Study of Twins Emphasizes Importance of Heredity." *Los Angeles Times.* October 12, 1990.

MacCambridge, Michael. "Why Women in Films Pick Jerky Boyfriends." Cox Newservice. July 1991.

Maccoby, Eleanor Emmons and Carol Nagy Jackin. *The Psychology of Sex Differences*. Palo Alto: Stanford University Press, 1974.

Majeski, William J. *The Lie Detection Book*. New York: Ballantine, 1991.

Markham, Howard, J. Quoted in "Talking Between The Sexes" by Leslie Drefous. *Los Angeles Times*. September 1990.

Martin, Linda and Seagrave, Kerry. *Women in Comedy: Funny Ladies from the Turn of the Century to the Present.* Citadel Press, 1986.

McEnroe, Colin. "All Pent Up." *Mirabella*. July 1990, p. 50.

McGill, Michael E. Ph.D. *The McGill Report on Male Intimacy*. New York: Holt, Rhinehart and Winston, 1985.

McWilliams, Peter and John-Roger. *Life 101*. Los Angeles: Prelude Press, 1991.

Meadors, Ellyn. "The Art of Complaining." *New Woman*. October 1990.

Menninger, Karl, M.D. *Love Against Hate*. New York: Harcourt, Brace & World, Inc., 1942.

Merlin, Katharine. "Sexual Jealousy." *Cosmopolitan*. October 1987.

Miller, Jean Baker. *Toward a New Psychology of Women*. Boston: Beacon Press, 1976.

Milwid, Beth, Ph.D. *Working With Men*. Oregon: Beyond Words, 1990.

Mitchell, Stephen. *Tao Te Ching*. New York: Harper & Row, Publishers, 1988.

Moir, Anne & David Jessel, *Brain Sex*. New York: Lyle Stuart, 1991.

Mornell, Pierre. *Passive Men, Wild Women*. New York: Ballantine, 1984.

Monthly Vital Statistics Report 39. (no. 7, suppl): 4, 1990.

Morris, Desmond. *Manwatching*. New York: Harry N. Abrams, Inc. 1977.

Naifeh, Steven & Gregory White Smith. *Why Can't Men Open Up*. New York: Clarkson N. Potter, Inc., 1984.

National Organization for Women, Seattle-King County NOW. *Woman, Assert Your Self!* New York: Harper & Row, 1976.

Nesbit, Lyn. "Men and Bimbos." *Self*. July 1990, p. 111.

Norwood, Robin. *Women Who Love Too Much*. New York: Pocket Books, 1985.

Notarius, C.I. & Johnson J. (1982) *Journal of Marriage and the Family*, 44, pp.483-489.

Peele, Stanton. *Love Addiction*. New York: New American Library, 1976.

Peck, M. Scott. M.D. *The Road Less Traveled*. New York: Simon & Schuster, 1978.

Person, Ethel S. "Some Differences Between Men and Women," *The Atlantic Monthly*. March 1988, p. 71-76.

Pfeiffer, Michelle, actress. Quoted in *New Women*. October 1990, p.20.

Pittman, Frank. M.D. "Chivalry for the '90's." *Networker*.

Nov./Dec. 1990

Pokela, Barbara. "Women See More to Life than Profits." *Minnesota-St. Paul Star Tribune*, 1990.

Prose, Francine. "Men May Fall for It, but Don't Be Shy and Sweet When You Talk with Them." *Self.* July 1991.

Pruett, Kyle D. Ph.D. *The Nurturing Father.* New York: Warner Books, 1987.

Quincy, Matthew. *Diet Right! A Consumer's Guide to Diet & Weight Loss Programs.* Berkeley CA: Conari Press, 1991.

Ralston, Jeannie. "Know Your Enemies." *Glamour.* August 1991.

Reagan, Nancy. "He Might Have Run Again" by Edward Klein. *Parade..* August 12, 1990.

Reiss, Bob. "The Answer Couple." *Glamour.* July 1990, p. 96.

Rhodes, Dr. Sonya and Dr. Marlin S. Potash. *Cold Feet: Why Men Don't Commit.* New York: Signet, 1989.

Rickard, Jacqueline. *Save Your Marriage Ahead of Time.* New York: M. Evans & Company, Inc. 1991.

Rinehart, Mary Roberts. *Isn't That Just Like A Man!* New York: George H. Doran Company, 1920.

Rosen, Ruth. "The Anti-War Gender Gap Is Back." *Los Angeles Times.* November 26, 1990.

Rubin, Dr. Lillian. *Just Friends.* New York: Harper & Row, 1985.

Safire, William. "A Bad Year for Women Around the World." *New York Times News Service. San Francisco Chronicle.* December 21, 1990.

Scarf, Maggie. *Intimate Partners.* New York: Ballantine, 1988.

Schaef, Anne Wilson. *Women's Reality.* San Francisco: Harper & Row Publishers, 1981.

Scheele, Dr. Adele. "The Flash Factor." *Working Woman.* September 1990, p.76.

_____ . "Male Bonding: Can you beat it? *Working Woman.* December 1990.

Seymour, Jane. "Not-So-Plain Jane Seymour." *The Saturday Evening Post.* May/June 1990.

Shaevitz, Marjorie. *The Superwomen Syndrome.* New York: Warner Books, 1984.

Siegel, Paula M. "Can You Psych Yourself Into Sex." *Self.* December 1990.

Sommers, Robert. Quoted in "More Men Seem to Have `Shopping Gene.'" By Faizah Alim. McClatchy News Service, July 25, 1991.

Stallone, Sylvester. "Rocky and Sly Goin Home," *San Francisco Chronicle*, October 26, 1990.

Starr, Tama. *The "Natural Inferiority" of Women: Outrageous Pronouncements by Misguided Males.* New York: Poseidon Press, 1991.

Stein, Harry. "Ask Harry." *Men's Life*, Fall 1990.

Stein, Ruthe. "At Last a Way to Talk To Your Mate." *San Francisco Chronicle.* September 1990.

_____ . "You Have To Know When To Give Up." *San Francisco*

Chronicle. October 1990.

Stein, Sara Bonnet. *Girls & Boys: The Limits of Nonsexist Childrearing.* New York: Charles Scribner's Sons, 1983.

Steinem, Gloria. "When Gloria Speaks...Women Listen" by Christine Wolfe, Gannet News Service. *Marin Independent Journal,* October 30, 1990.

____. "The Divinely Outspoken Ms. Steinem." *Cosmopolitan.* July 1990.

Stevens, Anthony. *The Roots of War.* New York: Paragon House. 1989.

Streep, Meryl. Actor. "TV and Film Actresses Seek Equal Pay." *USA Today,* August 2, 1990.

Stump, Jane Barr, Ph.D. *What's The Difference?* New York: William Morrow and Company, Inc., 1985.

Tanenbaum, Joe. *Male & Female Realities.* San Marcos, CA: Robert Erdmann Publishing, 1990.

Tannen, Deborah. *You Just Don't Understand.* New York: Ballantine, 1991.

____. *That's Not What I Meant.* New York: Ballantine, 1987.

Taylor, Carol and Markson, Elizabeth. "Interpretations of Older Women in Film: A Sociological and Psychological Analysis."

Thompson, Keith. *To Be a Man.* Los Angeles: Tarcher, 1991.

Toufexis, Anastasis. "Coming from a Different Place." *Time,* Fall 1990.

Ullman, Tracey. Quoted in *New Woman.* June 1989.

University of California, *Berkeley Wellness Letter.* "Codependency." June 1990, p.7.

Vedral, Joyce. *Boyfriends: Getting Them, Keeping Them, Living Without Them.* New York: Ballantine, 1990.

Wagenvoord, James. and Peyton Bailey. *Women: A Book For Men.* New York: Avon, 1979.

Waggoner, Susan. "Compulsive Eating & Sex." *Cosmopolitan.* August 1990.

Walker, Lenore. *The Battered Woman.* New York: HarperColophone Books, 1979.

Weiss, Daniel Evan. *The Great Divide: How Females & Males Really Differ.* New York: Poseidon Press, 1991.

Weitz, Shirley, *Nonverbal Communication.* New York: Oxford University Press, 1979.

Wesson, Carolyn. *Women Who Shop Too Much.* New York: St. Martin's Press, 1990.

West, Candace and Zimmerman, Don. "Sex Roles, Interruptions and Silences in Conversation." *Language and Dominance.* 105-129. Rowley, MA: Newbury House, 1975.

Whiting, B., and Pope, C. "A cross-culture analysis of sex differences in the behavior of children age three to eleven." *Journal of Social Psychology,* 1974.

White, Betty, Actor, Quoted in *New Woman.* June 1989.

Witelson, S.F. "Sex and the Single Hemisphere." *Science* 193
(1976) p. 425-427.
Wolf, Naomi. *The Beauty Myth*. New York: William Morrow and Co.,
Inc., 1991.
Wyer, E. Bingo. "50 Ideas To Put Snap Into Your Career."
Cosmopolitan. June 1991.
Yoder, Barbara. *The Recovery Resource Book*. New York: Fireside,
1990.
Zevin, Dan. "The Secret of Boys Clubs Revealed." *Self*. March 1990.
Zimmerman, Joy. "Men Who Abuse Women." *Pacific Sun*, April 1, 1988.

Find It Quickly